ROUTLEDGE · ENGLISH · TEXTS
GENERAL EDITOR · JOHN DRAKAKIS

ROBERT BROWNING
Selected Poetry and Prose

ROUTLEDGE · ENGLISH · TEXTS

GENERAL EDITOR · JOHN DRAKAKIS

Forthcoming

ROBERT BROWNING

Selected Poetry and Prose

Edited by Aidan Day

LONDON AND NEW YORK

First published 1991 by
Routledge
11 New Fetter Lane, London EC4P 4EE

Simultaneously published in the USA
and Canada by
Routledge
29 West 35th Street, New York,
NY 10001

Introduction, critical commentary
and notes © 1991 Aidan Day

Photoset by Rowland Phototypesetting Ltd
Bury St Edmunds, Suffolk
Printed in Great Britain by Clays Ltd
St Ives plc.

British Library Cataloguing in
Publication Data

Browning, Robert, 1812–1889
    Selected poetry and prose –
    (Routledge English texts)
    1. Title   II. Day, Aidan
    828.809

    ISBN 0-415-00952-9

Library of Congress Cataloging in
Publication Data

Browning, Robert, 1812–1889
    [Selections. 1991]
    Robert Browning: selected poetry and
        prose / edited by Aidan Day.
        – (Routledge English texts)
    Includes bibliographical references and
        index.
    ISBN 0-415-00952-9
    I. Day, Aidan.   II. Title. III. Series.
PR4203.D39   1991
821'.8 – dc20   90-46820

For my Mother and Father

Contents

ROBERT BROWNING: SELECTED POETRY AND PROSE

from **Dramatic Lyrics** (1842)

from **Dramatic Romances and Lyrics** (1845)

from **Men and Women** (1855)

from **Dramatis Personae** (1864)

Acknowledgements

For different kinds of advice on the preparation of this volume, I am very grateful to John Drakakis, Karina Williamson, Daniel Karlin, Kathryn Burlinson and, especially, Andrea Pentney.

Introduction

One of the best known of Browning's poems – '"Childe Roland to the Dark Tower Came"', first published in 1855 when Browning was 43 – is also one of his most enigmatic. In her *Handbook to the Works of Robert Browning* Mrs Sutherland Orr summarized the poem as the story of 'a brave knight performing a pilgrimage, in which hitherto all who attempted it have failed' (Orr 1896: p. 273). Below the 'surface' of the romance narrative, however, Mrs Orr found awkward 'discrepancies': 'as [Childe Roland] describes the country through which he passes, it becomes clear that half its horrors are created by his own heated imagination. . . . We can connect no idea of definite pursuit or attainment with a series of facts so dreamlike and so disjointed: still less extract from it a definite moral' (Orr 1896: pp. 273–4). The 'logic' of the narrative progression in '"Childe Roland"' is indeed less that of action in the external world than of the inner movement, the fluxes and refluxes, of the mind. Representation of literal action and landscape is transmuted throughout the poem into a figuring of psychological process. Thus, for example, in the ninth stanza, as Roland tells how at a certain stage of his journey he stepped from a road onto a surrounding plain, the road scene is immediately displaced in a manner that suggests the mysteriously arbitrary dynamic of reverie or dream-sequence:

> no sooner was I fairly found
> Pledged to the plain, after a pace or two,
> Than, pausing to throw backward a last view

1

O'er the safe road, 'twas gone; grey plain all round:
Nothing but plain to the horizon's bound.

Again, in stanza twenty-one, a description of the action of fording
a river is collapsed, without any explicit allegorical frame, into a
drama of disturbing psychological implication:

– It may have been a water-rat I speared,
    But, ugh! it sounded like a baby's shriek.

For the modern reader, used to the fragmentary and alogical
effects of much twentieth-century Modernist poetry, the disло-
cations and incertitudes of Browning's narrative may appear less
than surprising; even, perhaps, familiar. But it is not only that we
may recognize in Browning's work a highly individual antici-
pation of some aspects of Modernist poetic procedure. The
'discrepancies' in '"Childe Roland"' – those features of the poem
that seem most distinctively Browningesque – are distinctions
that at once signal Browning's place within a larger ideological
context.

That context is the legacy of the Romantic movement of the
late eighteenth and early nineteenth centuries. Romanticism –
with its various aesthetic and philosophical, social and political
dimensions – is a notoriously problematic phenomenon to define.
Nevertheless, the interiority of Browning's narrative in '"Childe
Roland"' calls to mind specifically that element in Romanticism
which Harold Bloom has characterized in terms of 'a revival of
romance':

> More than a revival, it is an internalization of romance,
> particularly of the quest variety, an internalization made . . .
> in the name of a humanizing hope that approaches apocalyp-
> tic intensity. . . . The movement of quest-romance, before
> its internalization by the High Romantics, was from nature to
> redeemed nature, the sanction of redemption being the gift of
> some external spiritual authority. . . . The Romantic move-
> ment is from nature to the imagination's freedom. . . . The
> quest is to widen consciousness as well as intensify it. . . .
> Wordsworth's Copernican revolution in poetry is marked by
> the evanescence of any subject but subjectivity.
>
> (Bloom 1971: pp. 15–16, 18)

2

The Romantic preoccupation with subjectivity, the celebration of the life of the individual mind, is far from a simple celebration of self-consciousness. Indeed, Romanticism typically finds in self-consciousness the root of the human experience of alienation in the world. A traditional religious view of human alienation – the Christian vision of a fall from paradisal union with God – is, as it were, secularized and internalized in Romantic thinking. In Romantic schemata, self-consciousness destroys wholeness and unity of being (or Being) as it divides the human mind from nature and also from itself. The malady of the human situation is located in the very distinction between subject and object that is the premise of self-consciousness. The mind that knows itself in distinction from the world is also the mind that, in its capacity to observe itself, stands always outside itself, caught in an endless recension of 'I's that watch other 'I's; a mind poised, as Wordsworth put it, 'On its own axis restlessly revolving' (*The Excursion*, IV. 629).

Where Christian thought had proposed a redemption for human kind deriving from an external spiritual source, the possibility of a making whole through the intervention of divine grace, Romanticism looked within the human mind itself for the capacity to overcome division and alienation. The name most frequently given to the potentially renovative and unifying resources of the mind was imagination. Something larger than either feeling or reason alone, the imagination was conceived as a cognitive faculty which enabled the human subject to apprehend absolute reality beyond the multiple appearances of the phenomenal world. As such a faculty the human imagination inhered in the very nature of the unitary reality which it grasped. In one of the most famous of Romantic formulas, Coleridge spoke of the 'primary IMAGINATION' as 'the living Power and prime Agent of all human Perception . . . a repetition in the finite mind of the eternal act of creation in the infinite I AM' (*Biographia Literaria*, Chapter 12). In this kind of thought – paralleled by Wordsworth when he spoke in *The Prelude* (1805: II. 272) of the human mind as 'an agent of the one great mind' – the individual human subject is identified with a transcendent subjectivity that is supposed to subsume the dualisms of self and other, of mind and nature, of subject and object. Subject, mind, or spirit, are given a priority over nature and matter, so that the forms of the material

3

world may be read as emblems of a profounder reality transcending nature, time and space. When Wordsworth relates, in the sixth book of *The Prelude*, how the 'Power' of 'Imagination' (1805: VI. 527, 525) rose within him during a journey across the Alps, he describes it as a power which revealed all natural forces to be something like the sign-language of the absolute:

> like workings of one mind, the features
> Of the same face, blossoms upon one tree,
> Characters of the great Apocalypse,
> The types and symbols of Eternity,
> Of first and last, and midst, and without end.
>
> (1805: VI. 568–72)

In Romantic thought, then, the tension between subject and object is resolved through positing an ultimate correlation between the individual mind and the mind of the absolute. It is an idealist resolution in favour of a totalized subjectivity, a totality which in some degree filled the space occupied by the divine in older religious systems of belief. It is in this sense that Romanticism was aptly characterized by T. E. Hulme as 'spilt religion' (Hulme 1924: p. 118). But there are, of course, problems here. While much Romantic writing expresses desire for continually renewed imaginative visions of what Coleridge called 'the one Life within us and abroad' ('The Eolian Harp', l. 26), it has of necessity to represent the complete realization of that vision as something potential rather than achieved. To realize the vision fully would be to pass beyond the bounds of individual life as well as beyond the writing which is itself constituted only within such bounds. Romantic poetic articulation thus repeatedly situates itself in a penultimate position. 'Our destiny, our nature, and our home / Is with infinitude' declares Wordsworth in *The Prelude* (1805: VI. 538–9) but that infinitude eludes the language that would speak of it:

> with infinitude, and only there;
> With hope it is, hope that can never die,
> Effort, and expectation, and desire,
> And something evermore about to be.
>
> (1805: VI. 539–42)

'Hope' and 'desire' and 'something evermore about to be'. Romantic psychology and metaphysics of the imagination turn on a principle of desire for absolute unity, and yet it is the principle of desire which reveals the inner contradictions of that psychology and metaphysics. Romanticism set itself the task of envisioning a dissolution of boundaries, a suspension of difference, a reconciliation of the split between subject and object. But it is, as Catherine Belsey has put it,

> the heroic impossibility of this task which produces Romantic exultation and despair. The obliteration of the object in a subjectivity which expands to incorporate it ('in our life alone does nature live' [Coleridge, 'Dejection: An Ode', l. 48]) is the negation of desire, because desire depends on the existence of an object that can be desired precisely in so far as it is outside the subject, radically other. The negation of desire, imaginary plenitude, presents a world whose existence and meaning depends on the presence of the subject, a world of absolute subjectivity. But the obliteration of the object implies the fading of the subject, because it is also the negation of difference.
>
> (Belsey 1986: pp. 68–9)

It is possible, then, to see a self-cancelling logic in Romantic yearning for a fullness that is to be achieved through overcoming division and incompleteness. The subjective plenitude proposed in Romantic notions of imaginative apocalypse – 'I have felt / A presence . . . / A motion and a spirit, that impels / All thinking things, all objects of all thought' (Wordsworth, 'Lines Composed a few miles above Tintern Abbey', ll. 94–5, 101–2) – locates only the reverse of what is proposed. The point of satisfying desire, the point of total synthesis, of realizing absolute subjectivity, would be the point at which subjectivity evaporates. The spirit that impels all objects of all thought disappears when it no longer has objects by which it may be distinguished and defined. Romantic exultation is generated in the desire for plenitude, but Romantic despair may be born of the recognition that the lack which constitutes the desire will in the last resort evacuate the plenitude it projects.

Exultation or, at least, steady confidence, are perhaps easily read in the work of such as Wordsworth. But glimmering despair

– a troubled comprehension of the evanescence of the subject –
emerge strikingly in the work of a younger Romantic such as
Shelley. On the one hand, in his essay 'A Defence of Poetry',
Shelley spoke enthusiastically of poetry as ' "the expression of the
imagination" ' and of the poet as one who 'participates in the
eternal, the infinite, and the one'. In this essay, Shelley adopts a
high Romantic confidence in the relevance to humanity of the
artist's subjective vision, though there is a significant wavering in
the way that he speaks of poets as the *unacknowledged* legislators of
the world' (my emphasis). In a poem such as 'Alastor', however,
Shelley explores a perception of the possible emptiness of any
projected total fulfilment of self. The 'Alastor' poet's yearning for
union with his own soul, for a dissolution of the gap between self
and other – figured in the vision of a 'veilèd maid' – turns into an
experience of possession by a 'fierce fiend of a distempered dream'
(ll. 151, 225). The poem is fraught with intimations of the lack
upon which desire is founded. They are intimations that threaten
throughout the poem to expose the Romantic celebration of an
ideal subjectivity as nothing more than a glamorization of
solipsistic vacancy. And it was this self-consciously threatened
ideology that was Browning's inheritance.

Browning was born in the London suburb of Camberwell on
7 May 1812; his mother, Sarah Anna (née Wiedemann), of
Scottish–German extraction; his father, Robert, a clerk in the
Bank of England. Taught to a large extent at home by professional tutors and by his father, Browning's education was informal
and unconventional. Above all, perhaps, he had access, in his
father's library, to a resource that was not only substantial (some
6,000 volumes) but eclectic and often obscure – a rich fund of
frequently eccentric detail in the literary, historical, and other arts
that first helped to shape and later continued to inform Browning's intellectual and imaginative tastes. It is tempting to draw a
parallel between the oddness of Browning's education and something that is almost a principle of his art. Isobel Armstrong has
commented on the way in which Browning's poetry can seem

> all Gothic frolic with minor historical figures, the poetry of an
> antiquarian with surprising streaks of energy, violence and
> intellectual sophistication. What unifying drive can one dis-
> cover among such diverse works as a poem about a medieval

quack philosopher (*Paracelsus*, 1835), or about an extremely minor poet caught up in the political struggles of pre-Dantean Italy (*Sordello*, 1840), a series of plays which are anything from the austere studies in political loyalty in *Strafford* (1837) to the overheated love-story unexpectedly embodied in a play with all the conventions of Victorian melodrama (*A Blot in the 'Scutcheon*, 1843), monologues spoken by mad dukes, Italian Renaissance painters, characters from Shakespeare and biblical characters?

(Armstrong 1969: p. 294)

Whatever the part played by Browning's early education and reading in the drive towards such poetic diversity, it is at least clear that his father's library was symptomatic of a family whose sympathies were structured, if not outside the terms of early nineteenth-century middle-class English culture, at any rate at odds with certain mainstream (Anglican and Tory) orthodoxies. It was a family aligned with religious dissent (Browning's mother, in particular, being a staunch Nonconformist) and with the politically liberal (Browning's father, as a young man, had given up a position on a West Indies sugar plantation, recoiling in horror from the slave system). For Browning, the family provided an early conditioning – ex-centric, not revolutionary – that was to show itself throughout his life and work.

Through his mother and her Nonconformist associations Browning came into contact with the Unitarian minister William Johnson Fox, whose circle was to form the basis of Browning's artistic and intellectual milieu during the years before he left England for Italy in 1846. Fox was a minister whose interests and commitments had been for some years drifting away from strict theology. In 1833 he reviewed Browning's first major poetic venture – the Shelleyan monodrama *Pauline* – in the *Monthly Repository*, a journal which he then edited as a vehicle of political and social reform, together with literary criticism. During the agitation for constitutional reform that had preceded the passing of the 1832 Reform Bill, Fox had been a prominent, even charismatic, spokesman for the liberal cause. Both Fox's spirituality and his politics were sensitive to the pulse of Romantic idealism and his general stance has invited comparison – even if not identification – with attitudes and emphases in Shelley:

Both held that evil was at most temporary. Both looked forward to a progress toward perfection. . . . Shelley's atheism was not incompatible with belief in a benevolent, all-pervading Spirit. Fox believed in a God of love. Both were hostile to conventions and institutions. Both maintained that men are basically good and that to be effectually good they need first of all to be free and equal.

(Irvine and Honan 1975: p. 29)

Fox not only gave *Pauline* the warmest notice it was to receive, but found a publisher for Browning's 1835 dramatic poem, *Paracelsus*, and introduced the young poet to Edward Moxon who would, in 1840, publish the historical narrative *Sordello*. The literary and intellectual circle that Fox opened up for Browning included John Forster, influential critic for the *Examiner*, and the actor W. C. Macready, whose suggestion in 1836 that Browning write a play for the stage prompted what was to turn into a series of plays that Browning produced between 1837 and 1846.

In his review of *Pauline* Fox commented on the way in which the poem shows 'Shelley . . . to have been the god' of Browning's 'early idolatry' (Litzinger and Smalley 1970: p. 36). Browning had indeed discovered Shelley's poems in 1826, and had taken with enthusiasm to some of the ideas and attitudes prevalent in those poems. But while Browning's intense early enthusiasm may have moderated, Shelley's influence over him was not something that was, in any simple sense, to pass. The three long poems which Browning wrote before 1840 – *Pauline*, *Paracelsus* and *Sordello* – all show him wrestling with the grand imaginative paradigms of Romantic ideology. So that at an early stage of *Paracelsus*, for example, we find Paracelsus endorsing Romantic idealist epistemology as he celebrates the *a priori* capacities of the mind:

> Truth is within ourselves; it takes no rise
> From outward things . . .
> There is an inmost centre in us all,
> Where truth abides in fulness . . .

(I. 726–9)

In *Pauline* Browning has his speaker reveal radical doubts about just such an idealism. In this work Browning insists on characterizing Shelley – almost apotheosized as the 'Sun-treader' – as a consummately confident idealist. But Browning has in fact noticed and is extending the scepticism concerning Romantic psychology and metaphysics that Shelley himself had at points manifested. In *Pauline* it simply serves Browning's purpose to construct Shelley and his work as an intact model against which the protagonist of *Pauline* may measure his own fallings off from certainty. The protagonist speaks as one considering retrospectively his difference from Shelley as he addresses in the present Shelley's supposedly still vital example:

> Sun-treader, life and light be thine for ever! . . .
> 　　　　　　　Remember me who flung
> All honour from my soul . . . and said . . .
> '. . . I have nought in common with him, shapes
> Which followed him avoid me, and foul forms
> Seek me, which ne'er could fasten on his mind . . .'
> 　　　　　　　　　　　　　　(151, 209–14)

Pauline, exploring a corrosive excess of self-conscious mental energy, recognizes the malign potencies of a fragmented psyche. But it is not only the baleful spectre of solipsism which haunts *Pauline*. The protagonist records a simultaneous loss of faith in a Romantic millenarian vision of social and political evolution, a loss of faith in a teleological view of history as the working out in time of an absolute spiritual and moral ideal:

> 　　　　　　　　I was vowed to liberty,
> Men were to be as gods and earth as heaven . . .
> 　　　　　　　　　　　　Now . . .
> I shall go mad, if I recall that time . . .
> First went my hopes of perfecting mankind,
> Next – faith in them, and then in freedom's self
> And virtue's self, then my own motives . . .
> 　　　　　　　　　(425–6, 428–9, 458–60)

By the end of the poem, the speaker, insisting that all is well again, reasserts an idealist programme which elides differing notions of transcendence as it co-opts at once the figure of Shelley and the more conventionally designated power of 'God':

> Sun-treader, I believe in God and truth
> And love . . .

I would lean on thee!
Thou must be ever with me, most in gloom
If such must come, but chiefly when I die,
For I seem, dying, as one going in the dark
To fight a giant: but live thou for ever . . .

(1020–1, 1023–7)

Despite the assertion of renewed confidence, however, the poem never exorcises the destructive forces of an unrelieved self-consciousness. The imaginative matrix of the poem resides in its engagement with division, as even the ominous closing images of gloom and warfare – counterpointing the statement of optimistic belief – reveal.

Likewise both *Paracelsus* and *Sordello* expose a radical dubiety concerning an idealizing and all-embracing 'Idea of the world'.[1] Paracelsus' conception of universal truth turns out to be exclusive and, while he remains convinced of the possibility of an inclusive vision, he ends with a recognition that his own blind will to achieve one has failed and that he has been: 'As . . . the over-radiant star too mad / To drink the life-springs, beamless thence itself' (V. 889–90). In *Sordello* historical contingency stubbornly contradicts and renders untenable an imaginative conception of ideal order in spiritual and temporal realms. The poem obsess-ively envisages not synthesis – of self and world, of imagination and history – but rather the shattering of relations, with the protagonist Sordello divided not least from himself:

Sordello vanished utterly,
Sundered in twain; each spectral part at strife
With each; one jarred against another life;
The Poet thwarting hopelessly the Man –

(II. 656–9)

Both *Paracelsus* and *Sordello* are wracked – as indeed, in their own modes, are Browning's poetic drama *Pippa Passes* (1841), the stage-plays of 1837–46, and even the testing of specifically Christian doctrine in *Christmas-Eve and Easter-Day* (1850) – between an impulse to affirm a unifying vision of personality and history, on the one hand, and a sense of the difficulty, perhaps the impossibility, of sustaining a totalizing vision of order, on the other. The unifying drive behind the variety of Browning's poetic subjects and treatments can be seen in terms of the poet's will to explore the ways in which human experience resists containment by any unifying drive.

Browning did not always use the long disquisitions of a *Pauline* or a *Sordello* to conduct this exploration. In his examination of the problematic relation between unity and diversity Browning adopted a range of shorter poetic forms. In particular, he developed kinds of poetry – the short dramatic lyric and monologue – that were more precisely sensitive to a sense of the breakdown of unitary world views, in general, and of Romantic unities of meaning and experience, in particular. Browning took the dramatic monologue, especially, to a level of sophistication that sometimes makes it seem as if he single-handedly invented the form. The present selection of Browning's verse concentrates on his short dramatic lyrics and monologues and the Critical Commentary at the end of this volume includes readings of individual works from this part of Browning's output.

Browning's early experiments in the short dramatic monologue appeared in 1836 when W. J. Fox published 'Porphyria's Lover' and 'Johannes Agricola in Meditation' in his *Monthly Repository*. These two poems were gathered, along with other examples of the dramatic monologue, in an 1842 volume entitled, plainly, *Dramatic Lyrics*. In 1844 and 1845 Browning contributed several poems – including the important monologue 'The Bishop Orders His Tomb at Saint Praxed's Church' – to *Hood's Magazine*. These, in turn, were gathered with other works in *Dramatic Romances and Lyrics*, published in 1845. But Browning's most remarkable single collection of short dramatic lyrics and monologues, the volume entitled *Men and Women*, was not to be published until 1855, nearly ten years after the most famously ex-centric happening of Browning's life – his elopement to Italy with Elizabeth Barrett.

When Browning and Elizabeth Barrett first met on 20 May 1845 she, some six years older than he, was also a considerably more widely recognized poet. Browning had first written to her in January 1845, expressing enthusiasm for her poetry and initiating a correspondence that would lead to their May meeting – with Elizabeth Barrett receiving Browning as she lay, semi-invalided, on a sofa in her father's house in Wimpole Street. The story of Elizabeth Barrett's life at home under the repressive regime of a possessive father, of the clandestine meetings with her lover and their exchange of emotionally highly charged letters, of their secret marriage (on 12 September 1846) and their escape by train from London to Southampton (19 September) and thence to Paris, has been rehearsed more times than some may care to remember. Yet for all its subsequent sentimentalization, the episode remains one of the most moving affairs in English literary history.[2]

The poets moved from Paris to Italy, where they lived initially at Pisa and from whence Elizabeth Barrett could write, in November 1846, 'I never was happy before in my life' (Kenyon 1897, I. 302). From Pisa the two moved in April 1847 to Florence, where they eventually found an apartment in the Casa Guidi that was to be their principal home for the duration of their married life and throughout the period Browning was writing the poems which made up *Men and Women*. Browning himself had never had significant financial means. He had lived largely in his parents' home until leaving England in 1846 and, while Elizabeth Barrett had some money of her own, for the earlier part of their marriage the two lived sometimes in straitened circumstances. In 1856, however, an old schoolfellow of Browning's father and a friend of Browning himself, John Kenyon, left the poets a substantial legacy. With their material embarrassments relieved the pair continued to live in Florence until, after a few days' illness, Elizabeth Barrett died in Browning's arms in the Casa Guidi apartment on 29 June 1861.

Following his wife's death, Browning returned to live in London and his poetic composition in the succeeding years continued unabated. In 1864 *Dramatis Personae* appeared, a volume which included poems – notably the monodrama 'James Lee's Wife' – written by Browning during summer sojourns in Brittany in 1862 and 1863. *Dramatis Personae* was followed by the publication of *The Ring and the Book* in 1868–9. *The Ring and the Book* is based on an account of a triple murder perpetrated in Rome in 1698 that was contained in an 'old yellow Book' (*The Ring and the Book*, I. 33) that Browning bought on a visit to Florence in 1860. The poem tells the murder story several times over from the different perspectives of those involved. Arranged in twelve books and nearly 22,000 lines long the work – usually regarded as the greatest of Browning's long poems – extends the implications of the dramatic monologue form as it raises fundamental issues of psychological and moral relativism.

The Ring and the Book marked Browning's greatest critical success to date; its reviewer for the *Athenaeum* declaring, for example, that the work 'is beyond all parallel the supremest poetical achievement of our time' (Litzinger and Smalley 1970: p. 317). It had not always been so. *Pauline* had been praised by one or two of Browning's acquaintances but remained obscure and unsold. *Paracelsus*, in contrast, received some warm notices; and reviews of Browning's first stage-play, *Strafford* (1837), were largely favourable – an exception to the rule of Browning's subsequent, largely unsuccessful, career as a playwright. With the publication of *Sordello* in 1840, however, disaster struck. Critics were almost unanimous in their animus towards the poem's convoluted syntax, its narrative prolixities, its recondite allusions. *Sordello* is, indeed, an extreme example of the characteristic difficulty of Browning's poetic mode. It is a mode that has always produced strongly hostile reactions – one of the most notable being that of George Santayana, who in 1900 published an essay entitled 'The Poetry of Barbarism' which attacked Browning's work as that of 'a thought and an art inchoate and ill–digested, of a volcanic eruption that tosses itself quite blindly and ineffectually into the sky' (Drew 1966: p. 18). Such a view continues occasionally to be heard in criticism even to the present day. But at the time of the publication of *Sordello* there were practically no countermanding views to alleviate the critical impact. The tenor of the general contemporary response to the poem is indicated by the *Metropolitan Magazine* which declared: 'We had rather write sonnets on the *latest*, as well as the earliest *speaking ass*, than be doomed to read such unintelligible oozings of nonsense'; or by the *Spectator*: 'digression, affectation, obscurity, and all the faults that spring . . . from crudity of plan and a self opinion which will neither cull thoughts nor revise composition' (Litzinger and Smalley 1970: pp. 66, 60). In a comparable, if more amused and amusing vein, Jane Welsh Carlyle observed, as Ian Jack has recounted, that she 'read the entire work without being able to make out whether Sordello was a man, a city, or a book' (Jack 1970: p. vii).

Browning was to live in the shadow of *Sordello* for some twenty years. While reception of his work was not unmitigatedly hostile during these years, it was quite sufficiently negative to direct Browning's address, in *The Ring and the Book*, to the 'British Public' as 'ye who like me not' (I. 410). Even *Men and Women* called forth predictable charges against a poetic mode that simply did not fit a prevailing aesthetic which held limpid mellifluousness in particularly high regard.[3] 'Our poets now speak in an unknown tongue' said the *Athenaeum* of *Men and Women* (Litzinger and Smalley 1970: pp. 155–6). 'We must . . . protest against his fashion . . . of continually running into absurd phrases and ridiculous rhymes . . . of perpetual obscurity where lucid statement is necessary' said the *Spectator* (Litzinger and Smalley 1970: p. 164). 'It is really high time that this sort of thing should, if possible, be stopped' said the *Saturday Review* (Litzinger and Smalley 1970, p. 158). But it wasn't possible. Not only was Browning not going to stop but 'forces were already at work which would raise him to popularity':

> at Oxford and Cambridge young men were beginning to 'discover' him. The Pre-Raphaelites, spurred by the exuberance of Dante Gabriel Rossetti, had been Browning devotees since 1847, and his poetry – not excluding the 'incomprehensible' *Sordello* – was read, argued over, and enthusiastically pressed on the attention of anyone who would listen. . . . the young intellectuals – the taste-makers of the next generation – had taken Browning to their bosoms, and the groundwork for his future fame was being laid.
>
> (Litzinger and Smalley 1970: p. 16)

That fame first began to break with the relatively good reception of Browning's three-volume *Poetical Works* of 1863, which collected poems from *Dramatic Lyrics*, *Dramatic Romances and Lyrics*, and *Men and Women*. The favourable notices of *Dramatis Personae* the following year preluded the eulogies which were to be heaped on *The Ring and the Book*. And during the last twenty years of Browning's life there came – with his increasing reputation as a poet – the social approbation sometimes accruing to literary fame. He was a much sought after dinner and house guest during the London season. A. S. Byatt has observed of this period of his life: 'He had to go to dinner parties, after his wife's death, to watch people, to stay alive. Henry James knew that there were two of him, the heartily sociable diner-out and the secret thinker-in-the-dark. People biographize the diner-out because he has left conventional traces. But it is the thinker-in-the-dark who is exciting'.[4] Browning was also the recipient of standard honorary recognitions of achievement: an LLD from Cambridge in 1879, DCL from Oxford in 1882, and LLD from Edinburgh in 1884. A literary celebrity and social lion, Browning continued to write copiously throughout these last twenty years and such works as *Fifine at the Fair* (1872) reveal intriguing flashes of brilliance. Yet successive generations of Browning readers have felt, with Lionel Trilling and Harold Bloom, that whatever his thinking, in the poetic practice of his later years Browning 'never again equalled' the 'greatest imaginings' of his work up to and including *The Ring and the Book*.[5] Nevertheless, by this time Browning's standing had risen almost to equal that of Tennyson and in 1881, with the founding of the Browning Society of London, the impetus to assimilate Browning to a Victorian pantheon of quasi-philosophical and ethical geniuses was given formal definition. When Browning died in Venice, on 12 December 1889, at the home of his son and only child, the process of canonization – notwithstanding those who continued to castigate the poet for his barbarous obscurity – was well under way.

NOTES

1 The expression is Matthew Arnold's, from a letter (?1848–9) to Arthur Hugh Clough (H. F. Lowry (ed.) (1932) *The Letters of Arthur Hugh Clough*, Oxford, Clarendon Press, p. 97).

2 The best account of the episode is given by Daniel Karlin in *The Courtship of Robert Browning and Elizabeth Barrett* (Karlin, 1985).

3 For discussions of Victorian poetic theory and taste see Robindra Kumar Biswas, 'The Question of Poetics', *Arthur Hugh Clough. Towards a Reconsideration* (Biswas, 1972); and Isobel Armstrong (ed.) *Victorian Scrutinies: Reviews of Poetry 1830 to 1870*, Armstrong, 1972.

4 'A. S. Byatt on Robert Browning', *Independent* Magazine, 26 November 1988, p. 78.

5 Lionel Trilling and Harold Bloom (eds) (1973) *The Oxford Anthology of English Literature, Victorian Poetry and Prose*, New York, London, Toronto, Oxford University Press, p. 493.

Chronology

1812   (7 May) Born in London suburb of Camberwell, the son of Robert Browning and Sarah Anna Browning (née Wiedemann).

c. 1820–6   Weekly boarder at the school of the Revd Thomas Ready in neighbouring Peckham. The main part of Browning's education, however, is acquired at home, with the aid of professional tutors, his parents, and his father's large and varied library.

c. 1824   Writes first volume of poems, entitled *Incondita*, which his parents try unsuccessfully to have published. Browning subsequently destroyed the volume and only two of the poems have survived.

1826   Reads Shelley.

1828   Enters the new University of London and stays for the most part of the academic year before withdrawing.

1832   (October) Browning sees Edmund Kean's performance of *Richard III*, stimulating his interest in theatre.

1833   (March) *Pauline* published anonymously to no sales and scant notice.

1834	(March–April) Considering a diplomatic career, Browning accompanies the Russian consul-general to St Petersburg.
1835	(October) *Paracelsus* published at his father's expense.
1836	(January) 'Johannes Agricola' and 'Porphyria' published in W. J. Fox's *Monthly Repository*. (May) Meets Wordsworth at a dinner given by the dramatist T. N. Talfourd; Macready invites Browning to write a play.
1837	(May) *Strafford*, Browning's first play, published and performed. With Macready taking the part of Strafford, it runs for five nights only at Covent Garden.
1838	(April–July) First visit to Italy.
1840	(March) *Sordello* published. The work is a serious failure, making Browning notorious for obscurity and retarding his critical reputation for more than twenty years.
1841	(April) *Pippa Passes*, Browning's second drama, appears as the first in a series of verse publications – eventually comprising eight pamphlets – issued under the general title *Bells and Pomegranates*.
1842	(March) *King Victor and King Charles*; a play published as *Bells and Pomegranates II*. (July) 'Essay on Chatterton', Browning's first extended critical prose piece, published anonymously in *Foreign Quarterly Review*. (November) *Dramatic Lyrics* published as *Bells and Pomegranates III*.
1843	(January and February) *The Return of the Druses* and *A Blot in the 'Scutcheon*, two plays published respectively as *Bells and Pomegranates IV* and *V*. *A Blot in the 'Scutcheon* is performed three times at Drury Lane, and fails.

1844	(April) *Colombe's Birthday*, a play published as *Bells and Pomegranates VI*.
	(Autumn) Visits Italy a second time.
1845	(10 January) Writes first letter to the poet Elizabeth Barrett ('I love your verses with all my heart . . .'), initiating an intense correspondence that will last throughout the period of their acquaintance, friendship and courtship.
	(20 May) Meets Elizabeth Barrett at her father's house, 50 Wimpole Street. The meeting is the first of many such, undertaken clandestinely to avoid the displeasure of Elizabeth Barrett's jealously possessive father.
	(November) *Dramatic Romances and Lyrics* published as *Bells and Pomegranates VII*
1846	(April) *Luria* and *A Soul's Tragedy*; two further dramas published as the eighth and last of the *Bells and Pomegranates* series.
	(12 September) Browning and Elizabeth Barrett marry secretly at St Marylebone Church.
	(19 September) Browning and Elizabeth Barrett elope, leaving England for Italy where they settle in Pisa.
1847	(April) The Brownings move to Florence, shortly taking an apartment in Casa Guidi which becomes, during their years of marriage, a permanent residence, varied by extended travels in Italy and sojourns in France and England.
1849	(January) *Poems* (2 volumes). The first collected edition of Browning's poems.
	(March) Birth of the Brownings' only child, Robert Wicdcmann Barrett ('Pen') Browning.
1850	(April) *Christmas-Eve and Easter-Day* published.
1851	(July–September) Browning makes first visit to London since marriage.
1852	'Essay on Shelley' published.

1855	(November) *Men and Women* published to un-enthusiastic reviews.
1856	The Brownings' financial problems relieved by an old friend, John Kenyon, who leaves them legacies amounting to £11,000 in his will.
1860	(June) Browning buys the 'old yellow Book', containing the seventeenth-century documents upon which he will base *The Ring and the Book*, at a bookstall in Florence.
1861	(29 June) Elizabeth Barrett dies. (August) Browning leaves Florence with his son. (October) Returns to live in London.
1862	(June) Settles at 19 Warwick Crescent, London.
1863	*The Poetical Works* (3 volumes) published.
1864	(May) *Dramatis Personae* published to warm critical acclaim. Browning lionized.
1867	Browning made Honorary MA of Oxford University and Honorary Fellow of Balliol College.
1868	*The Poetical Works* (6 volumes) published.
1868–9	(November–February) *The Ring and the Book* published and has extremely favourable reception.
1871	(August) *Balaustion's Adventures* published. (December) *Prince Hohenstiel-Schwangau* published.
1872	(June) *Fifine at the Fair* published.
1873	(May) *Red Cotton Night-Cap Country* published.
1875	(April) *Aristophanes' Apology* published. (November) *The Inn Album* published.
1876	(July) *Pacchiarotto and How He Worked in Distemper* published.
1877	(October) *The Agamemnon of Aeschylus* published.
1878	(May) *La Saisiaz; Two Poets of Croisic* published. First visit to Italy since death of his wife, establishing

a pattern of visits made almost every year until his death.

1879	(April) *Dramatic Idyls* published. Awarded LL D from Cambridge.
1880	(June) *Dramatic Idyls: Second Series* published.
1881	F. J. Furnivall founds the Browning Society (London).
1882	DCL from Oxford.
1883	(March) *Jocoseria* published.
1884	LL D from Edinburgh. (November) *Ferishtah's Fancies* published.
1887	(January) *Parleyings with Certain People of Importance in Their Day* published.
1888–9	*The Poetical Works* (16 volumes) published; the last collected edition supervised by Browning.
1889	(12 December) *Asolando* published. Browning dies on the evening of the same day in his son's house at Venice. (31 December) Buried in Poets' Corner, Westminster Abbey.
1894	*The Poetical Works*, volume 17, published; posthumously adding the poems from *Asolando* to the collected edition of 1888–9.

Textual Note

The poetical texts in this selection are based on the 1888–9 *Poetical Works* (Browning 1888–9) and incorporate Browning's emendations to the first printing of that edition (Kelley and Peterson 1973).

In his *Poems* (1849) Browning gathered poems published in *Dramatic Lyrics* (1842) and *Dramatic Romances and Lyrics* (1845) in their original order under the title 'Dramatic Romances and Lyrics'. The works from these two volumes were again gathered, together with poems from *Men and Women* (1855), in *The Poetical Works* (1863). In that 1863 collected edition, however, the poems from the 1842, 1845 and 1855 volumes were redistributed under three effectively new groupings entitled 'Lyrics', 'Romances' and 'Men, and Women'. This rearrangement was repeated in the collected editions of 1868 and 1888–9. While the texts of the present selection are based on the 1888–9 edition, the poems are presented under the title and according to the ordering of the original volume in which they appeared.

The passages from Browning's 'Essay on Shelley' are taken from the text of the essay edited in 1921 by H. F. B. Brett-Smith (Brett-Smith 1921). The extracts from Browning's letters to Elizabeth Barrett are taken from Daniel Karlin's edition of their correspondence (Karlin 1989). The extract from Browning's letter to John Ruskin is from E. T. Cook and A. Wedderburn's edition of *The Works of John Ruskin* (Cook and Wedderburn 1903–12).

ROBERT BROWNING
Selected Poetry and Prose

from
Dramatic Lyrics (1842)

MY LAST DUCHESS

Ferrara

That's my last Duchess painted on the wall,
Looking as if she were alive. I call
That piece a wonder, now: Frà Pandolf's hands
Worked busily a day, and there she stands.
Will't please you sit and look at her? I said
'Frà Pandolf' by design, for never read
Strangers like you that pictured countenance,
The depth and passion of its earnest glance,
But to myself they turned (since none puts by
The curtain I have drawn for you, but I)   10
And seemed as they would ask me, if they durst,
How such a glance came there; so, not the first
Are you to turn and ask thus. Sir, 'twas not
Her husband's presence only, called that spot
Of joy into the Duchess' cheek: perhaps
Frà Pandolf chanced to say 'Her mantle laps
Over my lady's wrist too much,' or 'Paint
Must never hope to reproduce the faint
Half-flush that dies along her throat:' such stuff
Was courtesy, she thought, and cause enough   20
For calling up that spot of joy. She had
A heart – how shall I say? – too soon made glad,
Too easily impressed; she liked whate'er

She looked on, and her looks went everywhere.
Sir, 'twas all one! My favour at her breast,
The dropping of the daylight in the West,
The bough of cherries some officious fool
Broke in the orchard for her, the white mule
She rode with round the terrace – all and each
Would draw from her alike the approving speech, 30
Or blush, at least. She thanked men, – good! but thanked
Somehow – I know not how – as if she ranked
My gift of a nine-hundred-years-old name
With anybody's gift. Who'd stoop to blame
This sort of trifling? Even had you skill
In speech – (which I have not) – to make your will
Quite clear to such an one, and say, 'Just this
Or that in you disgusts me; here you miss,
Or there exceed the mark' – and if she let
Herself be lessoned so, nor plainly set 40
Her wits to yours, forsooth, and made excuse,
– E'en then would be some stooping; and I choose
Never to stoop. Oh sir, she smiled, no doubt,
Whene'er I passed her; but who passed without
Much the same smile? This grew; I gave commands;
Then all smiles stopped together. There she stands
As if alive. Will't please you rise? We'll meet
The company below, then. I repeat,
The Count your master's known munificence
Is ample warrant that no just pretence 50
Of mine for dowry will be disallowed;
Though his fair daughter's self, as I avowed
At starting, is my object. Nay, we'll go
Together down, sir. Notice Neptune, though,
Taming a sea-horse, thought a rarity,
Which Claus of Innsbruck cast in bronze for me!

SOLILOQUY OF THE SPANISH CLOISTER

I

Gr-r-r – there go, my heart's abhorrence!
    Water your damned flower-pots, do!

If hate killed men, Brother Lawrence,
　　God's blood, would not mine kill you!
What? your myrtle-bush wants trimming?
　　Oh, – that rose has prior claims –
Needs its leaden vase filled brimming?
　　Hell dry you up with its flames!

II

At the meal we sit together:
　　Salve tibi! I must hear   10
Wise talk of the kind of weather,
　　Sort of season, time of year:
Not a plenteous cork-crop: scarcely
　　Dare we hope oak-galls, I doubt:
What's the Latin name for 'parsley'?
　　What's the Greek name for Swine's Snout?

III

Whew! We'll have our platter burnished,
　　Laid with care on our own shelf!
With a fire-new spoon we're furnished,
　　And a goblet for ourself,   20
Rinsed like something sacrificial
　　Ere 'tis fit to touch our chaps –
Marked with L. for our initial!
　　(He-he! There his lily snaps!)

IV

Saint, forsooth! While brown Dolores
　　Squats outside the Convent bank
With Sanchicha, telling stories,
　　Steeping tresses in the tank,
Blue-black, lustrous, thick like horsehairs,
　　– Can't I see his dead eye glow,   30
Bright as 'twere a Barbary corsair's?
　　(That is, if he'd let it show!)

V

When he finishes refection,
   Knife and fork he never lays
Cross-wise, to my recollection,
   As do I, in Jesu's praise.
I the Trinity illustrate,
   Drinking watered orange-pulp –
In three sips the Arian frustrate;
   While he drains his at one gulp.   40

VI

Oh, those melons? If he's able
   We're to have a feast! so nice!
One goes to the Abbot's table,
   All of us get each a slice.
How go on your flowers? None double?
   Not one fruit-sort can you spy?
Strange! – And I, too, at such trouble,
   Keep them close-nipped on the sly!

VII

There's a great text in Galatians,
   Once you trip on it, entails   50
Twenty-nine distinct damnations,
   One sure, if another fails:
If I trip him just a-dying,
   Sure of heaven as sure can be,
Spin him round and send him flying
   Off to hell, a Manichee?

VIII

Or, my scrofulous French novel
   On grey paper with blunt type!
Simply glance at it, you grovel
   Hand and foot in Belial's gripe: 60
If I double down its pages

At the woeful sixteenth print,
When he gathers his greengages,
　　Ope a sieve and slip it in't?

Or, there's Satan! – one might venture
　　Pledge one's soul to him, yet leave
Such a flaw in the indenture
　　As he'd miss till, past retrieve,
Blasted lay that rose-acacia
　　We're so proud of! *Hy, Zy, Hine* . . .   70
'St, there's Vespers! *Plena gratiâ*
　　Ave, Virgo! Gr-r-r – you swine!

JOHANNES AGRICOLA IN MEDITATION

There's heaven above, and night by night
　　I look right through its gorgeous roof;
No suns and moons though e'er so bright
　　Avail to stop me; splendour-proof
　　I keep the broods of stars aloof:
For I intend to get to God,
　　For 'tis to God I speed so fast,
For in God's breast, my own abode,
　　Those shoals of dazzling glory passed,
　　I lay my spirit down at last.   10
I lie where I have always lain,
　　God smiles as he has always smiled;
Ere suns and moons could wax and wane,
　　Ere stars were thundergirt, or piled
　　The heavens, God thought on me his child;
Ordained a life for me, arrayed
　　Its circumstances every one
To the minutest; ay, God said
　　This head this hand should rest upon
　　Thus, ere he fashioned star or sun.   20
And having thus created me,
　　Thus rooted me, he bade me grow,

29

Guiltless for ever, like a tree
   That buds and blooms, nor seeks to know
   The law by which it prospers so:
But sure that thought and word and deed
   All go to swell his love for me,
Me, made because that love had need
   Of something irreversibly
   Pledged solely its content to be.   30
Yes, yes, a tree which must ascend,
   No poison-gourd foredoomed to stoop!
I have God's warrant, could I blend
   All hideous sins, as in a cup,
   To drink the mingled venoms up;
Secure my nature will convert
   The draught to blossoming gladness fast:
While sweet dews turn to the gourd's hurt,
   And bloat, and while they bloat it, blast,
   As from the first its lot was cast.   40
For as I lie, smiled on, full-fed
   By unexhausted power to bless,
I gaze below on hell's fierce bed,
   And those its waves of flame oppress,
   Swarming in ghastly wretchedness;
Whose life on earth aspired to be
   One altar-smoke, so pure! – to win
If not love like God's love for me,
   At least to keep his anger in;
   And all their striving turned to sin.   50
Priest, doctor, hermit, monk grown white
   With prayer, the broken-hearted nun,
The martyr, the wan acolyte,
   The incense-swinging child, – undone
   Before God fashioned star or sun!
God, whom I praise; how could I praise,
   If such as I might understand,
Make out and reckon on his ways,
   And bargain for his love, and stand,
   Paying a price, at his right hand?   60

PORPHYRIA'S LOVER

The rain set early in to-night,
   The sullen wind was soon awake,
It tore the elm-tops down for spite,
   And did its worst to vex the lake:
   I listened with heart fit to break.
When glided in Porphyria; straight
   She shut the cold out and the storm,
And kneeled and made the cheerless grate
   Blaze up, and all the cottage warm;
   Which done, she rose, and from her form   10
Withdrew the dripping cloak and shawl,
   And laid her soiled gloves by, untied
Her hat and let the damp hair fall,
   And, last, she sat down by my side
   And called me. When no voice replied,
She put my arm about her waist,
   And made her smooth white shoulder bare,
And all her yellow hair displaced,
   And, stooping, made my cheek lie there,
   And spread, o'er all, her yellow hair,   20
Murmuring how she loved me – she
   Too weak, for all her heart's endeavour,
To set its struggling passion free
   From pride, and vainer ties dissever,
   And give herself to me for ever.
But passion sometimes would prevail,
   Nor could to-night's gay feast restrain
A sudden thought of one so pale
   For love of her, and all in vain:
   So, she was come through wind and rain.   30
Be sure I looked up at her eyes
   Happy and proud; at last I knew
Porphyria worshipped me; surprise
   Made my heart swell, and still it grew
   While I debated what to do.
That moment she was mine, mine, fair,
   Perfectly pure and good: I found
A thing to do, and all her hair

In one long yellow string I wound
    Three times her little throat around,
And strangled her. No pain felt she;
    I am quite sure she felt no pain.
As a shut bud that holds a bee,
    I warily oped her lids: again
    Laughed the blue eyes without a stain.
And I untightened next the tress
    About her neck; her cheek once more
Blushed bright beneath my burning kiss:
    I propped her head up as before,
    Only, this time my shoulder bore
Her head, which droops upon it still:
    The smiling rosy little head,
So glad it has its utmost will,
    That all it scorned at once is fled,
    And I, its love, am gained instead!
Porphyria's love: she guessed not how
    Her darling one wish would be heard.
And thus we sit together now,
    And all night long we have not stirred,
    And yet God has not said a word!

from
Dramatic Romances and Lyrics (1845)

HOME–THOUGHTS, FROM ABROAD

I

Oh, to be in England
Now that April's there,
And whoever wakes in England
Sees, some morning, unaware,
That the lowest boughs and the brushwood sheaf
Round the elm-tree bole are in tiny leaf,
While the chaffinch sings on the orchard bough
In England – now!

II

And after April, when May follows,
And the whitethroat builds, and all the swallows!   10
Hark, where my blossomed pear-tree in the hedge
Leans to the field and scatters on the clover
Blossoms and dewdrops – at the bent spray's edge –
That's the wise thrush; he sings each song twice over,
Lest you should think he never could recapture
The first fine careless rapture!
And though the fields look rough with hoary dew,
All will be gay when noontide wakes anew
The buttercups, the little children's dower
– Far brighter than this gaudy melon-flower!   20

THE BISHOP ORDERS HIS TOMB AT SAINT PRAXED'S CHURCH

Rome, 15—.

Vanity, saith the preacher, vanity!
Draw round my bed: is Anselm keeping back?
Nephews – sons mine . . . ah God, I know not! Well –
She, men would have to be your mother once,
Old Gandolf envied me, so fair she was!
What's done is done, and she is dead beside,
Dead long ago, and I am Bishop since,
And as she died so must we die ourselves,
And thence ye may perceive the world's a dream.
Life, how and what is it? As here I lie   10
In this state-chamber, dying by degrees,
Hours and long hours in the dead night, I ask
'Do I live, am I dead?' Peace, peace seems all.
Saint Praxed's ever was the church for peace;
And so, about this tomb of mine. I fought
With tooth and nail to save my niche, ye know:
– Old Gandolf cozened me, despite my care;
Shrewd was that snatch from out the corner South
He graced his carrion with, God curse the same!
Yet still my niche is not so cramped but thence   20
One sees the pulpit o' the epistle-side,
And somewhat of the choir, those silent seats,
And up into the aery dome where live
The angels, and a sunbeam's sure to lurk:
And I shall fill my slab of basalt there,
And 'neath my tabernacle take my rest,
With those nine columns round me, two and two,
The odd one at my feet where Anselm stands:
Peach-blossom marble all, the rare, the ripe
As fresh-poured red wine of a mighty pulse.   30
– Old Gandolf with his paltry onion-stone,
Put me where I may look at him! True peach,
Rosy and flawless: how I earned the prize!
Draw close: that conflagration of my church
– What then? So much was saved if aught were missed!
My sons, ye would not be my death? Go dig
The white-grape vineyard where the oil-press stood,

Drop water gently till the surface sink,
And if ye find . . . Ah God, I know not, I! . . .
Bedded in store of rotten fig-leaves soft,   40
And corded up in a tight olive-frail,
Some lump, ah God, of *lapis lazuli*,
Big as a Jew's head cut off at the nape,
Blue as a vein o'er the Madonna's breast . . .
Sons, all have I bequeathed you, villas, all,
That brave Frascati villa with its bath,
So, let the blue lump poise between my knees,
Like God the Father's globe on both his hands
Ye worship in the Jesu Church so gay,
For Gandolf shall not choose but see and burst!   50
Swift as a weaver's shuttle fleet our years:
Man goeth to the grave, and where is he?
Did I say basalt for my slab, sons? Black –
'Twas ever antique-black I meant! How else
Shall ye contrast my frieze to come beneath?
The bas-relief in bronze ye promised me,
Those Pans and Nymphs ye wot of, and perchance
Some tripod, thyrsus, with a vase or so,
The Saviour at his sermon on the mount,
Saint Praxed in a glory, and one Pan   60
Ready to twitch the Nymph's last garment off,
And Moses with the tables . . . but I know
Ye mark me not! What do they whisper thee,
Child of my bowels, Anselm? Ah, ye hope
To revel down my villas while I gasp
Bricked o'er with beggar's mouldy travertine
Which Gandolf from his tomb-top chuckles at!
Nay, boys, ye love me – all of jasper, then!
'Tis jasper ye stand pledged to, lest I grieve
My bath must needs be left behind, alas!   70
One block, pure green as a pistachio-nut,
There's plenty jasper somewhere in the world –
And have I not Saint Praxed's ear to pray
Horses for ye, and brown Greek manuscripts,
And mistresses with great smooth marbly limbs?
– That's if ye carve my epitaph aright,
Choice Latin, picked phrase, Tully's every word,

No gaudy ware like Gandolf's second line –
Tully, my masters? Ulpian serves his need!
And then how I shall lie through centuries, 80
And hear the blessed mutter of the mass,
And see God made and eaten all day long,
And feel the steady candle-flame, and taste
Good strong thick stupefying incense-smoke!
For as I lie here, hours of the dead night,
Dying in state and by such slow degrees,
I fold my arms as if they clasped a crook,
And stretch my feet forth straight as stone can point,
And let the bedclothes, for a mortcloth, drop
Into great laps and folds of sculptor's-work: 90
And as yon tapers dwindle, and strange thoughts
Grow, with a certain humming in my ears,
About the life before I lived this life,
And this life too, popes, cardinals and priests,
Saint Praxed at his sermon on the mount,
Your tall pale mother with her talking eyes,
And new-found agate urns as fresh as day,
And marble's language, Latin pure, discreet,
– Aha, ELUCESCEBAT quoth our friend?
No Tully, said I, Ulpian at the best! 100
Evil and brief hath been my pilgrimage.
All *lapis*, all, sons! Else I give the Pope
My villas! Will ye ever eat my heart?
Ever your eyes were as a lizard's quick,
They glitter like your mother's for my soul,
Or ye would heighten my impoverished frieze,
Piece out its starved design, and fill my vase
With grapes, and add a vizor and a Term,
And to the tripod ye would tie a lynx
That in his struggle throws the thyrsus down, 110
To comfort me on my entablature
Whereon I am to lie till I must ask
'Do I live, am I dead?' There, leave me, there!
For ye have stabbed me with ingratitude
To death – ye wish it – God, ye wish it! Stone –
Gritstone, a-crumble! Clammy squares which sweat
As if the corpse they keep were oozing through –

And no more *lapis* to delight the world!
Well go! I bless ye. Fewer tapers there,
But in a row: and, going, turn your backs   120
– Ay, like departing altar-ministrants,
And leave me in my church, the church for peace,
That I may watch at leisure if he leers –
Old Gandolf, at me, from his onion-stone,
As still he envied me, so fair she was!

from
Men and Women (1855)

LOVE AMONG THE RUINS

I

Where the quiet-coloured end of evening smiles,
    Miles and miles
On the solitary pastures where our sheep
    Half-asleep
Tinkle homeward thro' the twilight, stray or stop
    As they crop –
Was the site once of a city great and gay,
    (So they say)
Of our country's very capital, its prince
    Ages since   10
Held his court in, gathered councils, wielding far
    Peace or war.

II

Now, – the country does not even boast a tree,
    As you see,
To distinguish slopes of verdure, certain rills
    From the hills
Intersect and give a name to, (else they run
    Into one)
Where the domed and daring palace shot its spires
    Up like fires   20

O'er the hundred-gated circuit of a wall
   Bounding all,
Made of marble, men might march on nor be pressed,
   Twelve abreast.

III

And such plenty and perfection, see, of grass
   Never was!
Such a carpet as, this summer-time, o'erspreads
   And embeds
Every vestige of the city, guessed alone,
   Stock or stone –   30
Where a multitude of men breathed joy and woe
   Long ago;
Lust of glory pricked their hearts up, dread of shame
   Struck them tame;
And that glory and that shame alike, the gold
   Bought and sold.

IV

Now, – the single little turret that remains
   On the plains,
By the caper overrooted, by the gourd
   Overscored,   40
While the patching houseleek's head of blossom winks
   Through the chinks –
Marks the basement whence a tower in ancient time
   Sprang sublime,
And a burning ring, all round, the chariots traced
   As they raced,
And the monarch and his minions and his dames
   Viewed the games.

V

And I know, while thus the quiet-coloured eve
   Smiles to leave   50

To their folding, all our many-tinkling fleece
    In such peace,
And the slopes and rills in undistinguished grey
    Melt away –
That a girl with eager eyes and yellow hair
    Waits me there
In the turret whence the charioteers caught soul
    For the goal,
When the king looked, where she looks now, breathless, dumb
    Till I come.   60

VI

But he looked upon the city, every side,
    Far and wide,
All the mountains topped with temples, all the glades'
    Colonnades,
All the causeys, bridges, aqueducts, – and then,
    All the men!
When I do come, she will speak not, she will stand,
    Either hand
On my shoulder, give her eyes the first embrace
    Of my face,   70
Ere we rush, ere we extinguish sight and speech
    Each on each

VII

In one year they sent a million fighters forth
    South and North,
And they built their gods a brazen pillar high
    As the sky,
Yet reserved a thousand chariots in full force –
    Gold, of course.
Oh heart! oh blood that freezes, blood that burns!
    Earth's returns   80
For whole centuries of folly, noise and sin!
    Shut them in,

40

With their triumphs and their glories and the rest!
   Love is best.

I am poor brother Lippo, by your leave!
You need not clap your torches to my face.
Zooks, what's to blame? you think you see a monk!
What, 'tis past midnight, and you go the rounds,
And here you catch me at an alley's end
Where sportive ladies leave their doors ajar?
The Carmine's my cloister: hunt it up,
Do, – harry out, if you must show your zeal,
Whatever rat, there, haps on his wrong hole,
And nip each softling of a wee white mouse,   10
Weke, weke, that's crept to keep him company!
Aha, you know your betters! Then, you'll take
Your hand away that's fiddling on my throat,
And please to know me likewise. Who am I?
Why, one, sir, who is lodging with a friend
Three streets off – he's a certain . . . how d'ye call?
Master – a . . . Cosimo of the Medici,
I' the house that caps the corner. Boh! you were best!
Remember and tell me, the day you're hanged,
How you affected such a gullet's-gripe!   20
But you, sir, it concerns you that your knaves
Pick up a manner nor discredit you:
Zooks, are we pilchards, that they sweep the streets
And count fair prize what comes into their net?
He's Judas to a tittle, that man is!
Just such a face! Why, sir, you make amends.
Lord, I'm not angry! Bid your hangdogs go
Drink out this quarter-florin to the health
Of the munificent House that harbours me
(And many more beside, lads! more beside!)   30
And all's come square again. I'd like his face –
His, elbowing on his comrade in the door
With the pike and lantern, – for the slave that holds
John Baptist's head a-dangle by the hair
With one hand ('Look you, now,' as who should say)

And his weapon in the other, yet unwiped!
It's not your chance to have a bit of chalk,
A wood-coal or the like? or you should see!
Yes, I'm the painter, since you style me so.
What, brother Lippo's doings, up and down,   40
You know them and they take you? like enough!
I saw the proper twinkle in your eye –
'Tell you, I liked your looks at very first.
Let's sit and set things straight now, hip to haunch.
Here's spring come, and the nights one makes up bands
To roam the town and sing out carnival,
And I've been three weeks shut within my mew,
A-painting for the great man, saints and saints
And saints again. I could not paint all night –
Ouf! I leaned out of window for fresh air.   50
There came a hurry of feet and little feet,
A sweep of lute-strings, laughs, and whifts of song, –
Flower o' the broom,
Take away love, and our earth is a tomb!
Flower o' the quince,
I let Lisa go, and what good in life since?
Flower o' the thyme – and so on. Round they went.
Scarce had they turned the corner when a titter
Like the skipping of rabbits by moonlight, – three slim
    shapes,
And a face that looked up . . . zooks, sir, flesh and blood,   60
That's all I'm made of! Into shreds it went,
Curtain and counterpane and coverlet,
All the bed-furniture – a dozen knots,
There was a ladder! Down I let myself,
Hands and feet, scrambling somehow, and so dropped,
And after them. I came up with the fun
Hard by Saint Laurence, hail fellow, well met, –
Flower o' the rose,
If I've been merry, what matter who knows?
And so as I was stealing back again   70
To get to bed and have a bit of sleep
Ere I rise up to-morrow and go work
On Jerome knocking at his poor old breast
With his great round stone to subdue the flesh,

42

You snap me of the sudden. Ah, I see!
Though your eye twinkles still, you shake your head –
Mine's shaved – a monk, you say – the sting's in that!
If Master Cosimo announced himself,
Mum's the word naturally; but a monk!
Come, what am I a beast for? tell us, now!   80
I was a baby when my mother died
And father died and left me in the street.
I starved there, God knows how, a year or two
On fig-skins, melon-parings, rinds and shucks,
Refuse and rubbish. One fine frosty day,
My stomach being empty as your hat,
The wind doubled me up and down I went.
Old Aunt Lapaccia trussed me with one hand,
(Its fellow was a stinger as I knew)
And so along the wall, over the bridge,   90
By the straight cut to the convent. Six words there,
While I stood munching my first bread that month:
'So, boy, you're minded,' quoth the good fat father
Wiping his own mouth, 'twas refection-time, –
'To quit this very miserable world?
Will you renounce' . . . 'the mouthful of bread?' thought I;
By no means! Brief, they made a monk of me;
I did renounce the world, its pride and greed,
Palace, farm, villa, shop and banking-house,
Trash, such as these poor devils of Medici   100
Have given their hearts to – all at eight years old.
Well, sir, I found in time, you may be sure,
'Twas not for nothing – the good bellyful,
The warm serge and the rope that goes all round,
And day-long blessed idleness beside!
'Let's see what the urchin's fit for' – that came next.
Not overmuch their way, I must confess.
Such a to-do! They tried me with their books:
Lord, they'd have taught me Latin in pure waste!
Flower o' the clove,   110
All the Latin I construe is, 'amo' I love!
But, mind you, when a boy starves in the streets
Eight years together, as my fortune was,
Watching folk's faces to know who will fling

The bit of half-stripped grape-bunch he desires,
And who will curse or kick him for his pains, –
Which gentleman processional and fine,
Holding a candle to the Sacrament,
Will wink and let him lift a plate and catch
The droppings of the wax to sell again,   120
Or holla for the Eight and have him whipped, –
How say I? – nay, which dog bites, which lets drop
His bone from the heap of offal in the street, –
Why, soul and sense of him grow sharp alike,
He learns the look of things, and none the less
For admonition from the hunger-pinch.
I had a store of such remarks, be sure,
Which, after I found leisure, turned to use.
I drew men's faces on my copy-books,
Scrawled them within the antiphonary's marge,   130
Joined legs and arms to the long music-notes,
Found eyes and nose and chin for A's and B's,
And made a string of pictures of the world
Betwixt the ins and outs of verb and noun,
On the wall, the bench, the door. The monks looked
     black.
'Nay,' quoth the Prior, 'turn him out, d'ye say?
In no wise. Lose a crow and catch a lark.
What if at last we get our man of parts,
We Carmelites, like those Camaldolese
And Preaching Friars, to do our church up fine   140
And put the front on it that ought to be!'
And hereupon he bade me daub away.
Thank you! my head being crammed, the walls a blank,
Never was such prompt disemburdening.
First, every sort of monk, the black and white,
I drew them, fat and lean: then, folk at church,
From good old gossips waiting to confess
Their cribs of barrel-droppings, candle-ends, –
To the breathless fellow at the altar-foot,
Fresh from his murder, safe and sitting there   150
With the little children round him in a row
Of admiration, half for his beard and half
For that white anger of his victim's son

Shaking a fist at him with one fierce arm,
Signing himself with the other because of Christ
(Whose sad face on the cross sees only this
After the passion of a thousand years)
Till some poor girl, her apron o'er her head,
(Which the intense eyes looked through) came at eve
On tiptoe, said a word, dropped in a loaf,   160
Her pair of earrings and a bunch of flowers
(The brute took growling), prayed, and so was gone.
I painted all, then cried ' 'Tis ask and have;
Choose, for more's ready!' – laid the ladder flat,
And showed my covered bit of cloister-wall.
The monks closed in a circle and praised loud
Till checked, taught what to see and not to see,
Being simple bodies, – 'That's the very man!
Look at the boy who stoops to pat the dog!
That woman's like the Prior's niece who comes   170
To care about his asthma: it's the life!'
But there my triumph's straw-fire flared and funked;
Their betters took their turn to see and say:
The Prior and the learned pulled a face
And stopped all that in no time. 'How? what's here?
Quite from the mark of painting, bless us all!
Faces, arms, legs and bodies like the true
As much as pea and pea! it's devil's-game!
Your business is not to catch men with show,
With homage to the perishable clay,   180
But lift them over it, ignore it all,
Make them forget there's such a thing as flesh.
Your business is to paint the souls of men –
Man's soul, and it's a fire, smoke . . . no, it's not . . .
It's vapour done up like a new-born babe –
(In that shape when you die it leaves your mouth)
It's . . . well, what matters talking, it's the soul!
Give us no more of body than shows soul!
Here's Giotto, with his Saint a-praising God,
That sets us praising, – why not stop with him?   190
Why put all thoughts of praise out of our head
With wonder at lines, colours, and what not?
Paint the soul, never mind the legs and arms!

Rub all out, try at it a second time.
Oh, that white smallish female with the breasts,
She's just my niece . . . Herodias, I would say, –
Who went and danced and got men's heads cut off!
Have it all out!' Now, is this sense, I ask?
A fine way to paint soul, by painting body
So ill, the eye can't stop there, must go further   200
And can't fare worse! Thus, yellow does for white
When what you put for yellow's simply black,
And any sort of meaning looks intense
When all beside itself means and looks nought.
Why can't a painter lift each foot in turn,
Left foot and right foot, go a double step,
Make his flesh liker and his soul more like,
Both in their order? Take the prettiest face,
The Prior's niece . . . patron-saint – is it so pretty
You can't discover if it means hope, fear,   210
Sorrow or joy? won't beauty go with these?
Suppose I've made her eyes all right and blue,
Can't I take breath and try to add life's flash,
And then add soul and heighten them threefold?
Or say there's beauty with no soul at all –
(I never saw it – put the case the same –)
If you get simple beauty and nought else,
You get about the best thing God invents:
That's somewhat: and you'll find the soul you have missed,
Within yourself, when you return him thanks.   220
'Rub all out!' Well, well, there's my life, in short,
And so the thing has gone on ever since.
I'm grown a man no doubt, I've broken bounds:
You should not take a fellow eight years old
And make him swear to never kiss the girls.
I'm my own master, paint now as I please –
Having a friend, you see, in the Corner-house!
Lord, it's fast holding by the rings in front –
Those great rings serve more purposes than just
To plant a flag in, or tie up a horse!   230
And yet the old schooling sticks, the old grave eyes
Are peeping o'er my shoulder as I work,

The heads shake still – 'It's art's decline, my son!
You're not of the true painters, great and old;
Brother Angelico's the man, you'll find;
Brother Lorenzo stands his single peer:
Fag on at flesh, you'll never make the third!'
Flower o' the pine,
You keep your mistr . . . manners, and I'll stick to mine!
I'm not the third, then: bless us, they must know!   240
Don't you think they're the likeliest to know,
They with their Latin? So, I swallow my rage,
Clench my teeth, suck my lips in tight, and paint
To please them – sometimes do and sometimes don't;
For, doing most, there's pretty sure to come
A turn, some warm eve finds me at my saints –
A laugh, a cry, the business of the world –
(*Flower o' the peach,*
Death for us all, and his own life for each!)
And my whole soul revolves, the cup runs over,   250
The world and life's too big to pass for a dream,
And I do these wild things in sheer despite,
And play the fooleries you catch me at,
In pure rage! The old mill-horse, out at grass
After hard years, throws up his stiff heels so,
Although the miller does not preach to him
The only good of grass is to make chaff.
What would men have? Do they like grass or no –
May they or mayn't they? all I want's the thing
Settled for ever one way. As it is,   260
You tell too many lies and hurt yourself:
You don't like what you only like too much,
You do like what, if given you at your word,
You find abundantly detestable.
For me, I think I speak as I was taught;
I always see the garden and God there
A-making man's wife: and, my lesson learned,
The value and significance of flesh,
I can't unlearn ten minutes afterwards.

    You understand me: I'm a beast, I know.   270
But see, now – why, I see as certainly

As that the morning-star's about to shine,
What will hap some day. We've a youngster here
Comes to our convent, studies what I do,
Slouches and stares and lets no atom drop:
His name is Guidi – he'll not mind the monks –
They call him Hulking Tom, he lets them talk –
He picks my practice up – he'll paint apace,
I hope so – though I never live so long,
I know what's sure to follow. You be judge!   280
You speak no Latin more than I, belike;
However, you're my man, you've seen the world
– The beauty and the wonder and the power,
The shapes of things, their colours, lights and shades,
Changes, surprises, – and God made it all!
– For what? Do you feel thankful, ay or no,
For this fair town's face, yonder river's line,
The mountain round it and the sky above,
Much more the figures of man, woman, child,
These are the frame to? What's it all about?   290
To be passed over, despised? or dwelt upon,
Wondered at? oh, this last of course! – you say.
But why not do as well as say, – paint these
Just as they are, careless what comes of it?
God's works – paint anyone, and count it crime
To let a truth slip. Don't object, 'His works
Are here already; nature is complete:
Suppose you reproduce her – (which you can't)
There's no advantage! you must beat her, then.'
For, don't you mark? we're made so that we love   300
First when we see them painted, things we have passed
Perhaps a hundred times nor cared to see;
And so they are better, painted – better to us,
Which is the same thing. Art was given for that;
God uses us to help each other so,
Lending our minds out. Have you noticed, now,
Your cullion's hanging face? A bit of chalk,
And trust me but you should, though! How much more,
If I drew higher things with the same truth!
That were to take the Prior's pulpit-place,   310
Interpret God to all of you! Oh, oh,

It makes me mad to see what men shall do
And we in our graves! This world's no blot for us,
Nor blank; it means intensely, and means good:
To find its meaning is my meat and drink.
'Ay, but you don't so instigate to prayer!'
Strikes in the Prior: 'when your meaning's plain
It does not say to folk – remember matins,
Or, mind you fast next Friday!' Why, for this
What need of art at all? A skull and bones,   320
Two bits of stick nailed crosswise, or, what's best,
A bell to chime the hour with, does as well.
I painted a Saint Laurence six months since
At Prato, splashed the fresco in fine style:
'How looks my painting, now the scaffold's down?'
I ask a brother: 'Hugely,' he returns –
'Already not one phiz of your three slaves
Who turn the Deacon off his toasted side,
But's scratched and prodded to our heart's content,
The pious people have so eased their own   330
With coming to say prayers there in a rage:
We get on fast to see the bricks beneath.
Expect another job this time next year,
For pity and religion grow i' the crowd –
Your painting serves its purpose!' Hang the fools!

   – That is – you'll not mistake an idle word
Spoke in a huff by a poor monk, God wot,
Tasting the air this spicy night which turns
The unaccustomed head like Chianti wine!
Oh, the church knows! don't misreport me, now!   340
It's natural a poor monk out of bounds
Should have his apt word to excuse himself:
And hearken how I plot to make amends.
I have bethought me: I shall paint a piece
. . . There's for you! Give me six months, then go, see
Something in Sant' Ambrogio's! Bless the nuns!
They want a cast o' my office. I shall paint
God in the midst, Madonna and her babe,
Ringed by a bowery flowery angel-brood,
Lilies and vestments and white faces, sweet   350

49

As puff on puff of grated orris-root
When ladies crowd to Church at midsummer.
And then i' the front, of course a saint or two –
Saint John, because he saves the Florentines,
Saint Ambrose, who puts down in black and white
The convent's friends and gives them a long day,
And Job, I must have him there past mistake,
The man of Uz (and Us without the z,
Painters who need his patience). Well, all these
Secured at their devotion, up shall come   360
Out of a corner when you least expect,
As one by a dark stair into a great light,
Music and talking, who but Lippo! I! –
Mazed, motionless and moonstruck – I'm the man!
Back I shrink – what is this I see and hear?
I, caught up with my monk's-things by mistake,
My old serge gown and rope that goes all round,
I, in this presence, this pure company!
Where's a hole, where's a corner for escape?
Then steps a sweet angelic slip of a thing   370
Forward, puts out a soft palm – 'Not so fast!'
– Addresses the celestial presence, 'nay –
He made you and devised you, after all,
Though he's none of you! Could Saint John there draw –
His camel-hair make up a painting-brush?
We come to brother Lippo for all that,
Iste perfecit opus!' So, all smile –
I shuffle sideways with my blushing face
Under the cover of a hundred wings
Thrown like a spread of kirtles when you're gay   380
And play hot cockles, all the doors being shut,
Till, wholly unexpected, in there pops
The hothead husband! Thus I scuttle off
To some safe bench behind, not letting go
The palm of her, the little lily thing
That spoke the good word for me in the nick,
Like the Prior's niece . . . Saint Lucy, I would say.
And so all's saved for me, and for the church
A pretty picture gained. Go, six months hence!
Your hand, sir, and good-bye: no lights, no lights!   390

50

The street's hushed, and I know my own way back,
Don't fear me! There's the grey beginning. Zooks!

A TOCCATA OF GALUPPI'S

I

Oh Galuppi, Baldassaro, this is very sad to find!
I can hardly misconceive you; it would prove me deaf and
    blind;
But although I take your meaning, 'tis with such a heavy
    mind!

II

Here you come with your old music, and here's all the
    good it brings.
What, they lived once thus at Venice where the merchants
    were the kings,
Where Saint Mark's is, where the Doges used to wed the
    sea with rings?

III

Ay, because the sea's the street there; and 'tis arched by
    . . . what you call
. . . Shylock's bridge with houses on it, where they kept
    the carnival:
I was never out of England – it's as if I saw it all.

IV

Did young people take their pleasure when the sea was
    warm in May?   10
Balls and masks begun at midnight, burning ever to
    mid-day,
When they made up fresh adventures for the morrow, do
    you say?

Was a lady such a lady, cheeks so round and lips so red, –
On her neck the small face buoyant, like a bell-flower on
its bed,
O'er the breast's superb abundance where a man might
base his head?

Well, and it was graceful of them – they'd break talk off
and afford
– She, to bite her mask's black velvet – he, to finger on his
sword,
While you sat and played Toccatas, stately at the
clavichord?

What? Those lesser thirds so plaintive, sixths diminished,
sigh on sigh,
Told them something? Those suspensions, those solutions
– 'Must we die?'   20
Those commiserating sevenths – 'Life might last! we can
but try!'

'Were you happy?' – 'Yes.' – 'And are you still as happy?' –
'Yes. And you?'
– 'Then, more kisses!' – 'Did I stop them, when a million
seemed so few?'
Hark, the dominant's persistence till it must be answered
to!

So, an octave struck the answer. Oh, they praised you, I
dare say!
'Brave Galuppi! that was music! good alike at grave and
gay!
I can always leave off talking when I hear a master play!'

X

Then they left you for their pleasure: till in due time, one
    by one,
Some with lives that came to nothing, some with deeds as
    well undone,
Death stepped tacitly and took them where they never see
    the sun.   30

XI

But when I sit down to reason, think to take my stand nor
    swerve,
While I triumph o'er a secret wrung from nature's close
    reserve,
In you come with your cold music till I creep through
    every nerve.

XII

Yes, you, like a ghostly cricket, creaking where a house
    was burned:
'Dust and ashes, dead and done with, Venice spent what
    Venice earned.
The soul, doubtless, is immortal – where a soul can be
    discerned.

XIII

'Yours for instance: you know physics, something of
    geology,
Mathematics are your pastime; souls shall rise in their
    degree;
Butterflies may dread extinction, – you'll not die, it cannot
    be!

XIV

'As for Venice and her people, merely born to bloom and
    drop,   40

Here on earth they bore their fruitage, mirth and folly
    were the crop:
What of soul was left, I wonder, when the kissing had to
    stop?

XV

'Dust and ashes!' So you creak it, and I want the heart to
    scold.
Dear dead women, with such hair, too – what's become of
    all the gold
Used to hang and brush their bosoms? I feel chilly and
    grown old.

BY THE FIRE–SIDE

I

How well I know what I mean to do
    When the long dark autumn-evenings come;
And where, my soul, is thy pleasant hue?
    With the music of all thy voices, dumb
In life's November too!

II

I shall be found by the fire, suppose,
    O'er a great wise book as beseemeth age,
While the shutters flap as the cross-wind blows
    And I turn the page, and I turn the page,
Not verse now, only prose!   10

III

Till the young ones whisper, finger on lip,
    'There he is at it, deep in Greek:
Now then, or never, out we slip
    To cut from the hazels by the creek
A mainmast for our ship!'

IV

I shall be at it indeed, my friends:
    Greek puts already on either side
Such a branch-work forth as soon extends
    To a vista opening far and wide,
And I pass out where it ends.   20

V

The outside-frame, like your hazel-trees:
    But the inside-archway widens fast,
And a rarer sort succeeds to these,
    And we slope to Italy at last
And youth, by green degrees.

VI

I follow wherever I am led,
    Knowing so well the leader's hand:
Oh woman-country, wooed not wed,
    Loved all the more by earth's male-lands,
Laid to their hearts instead!   30

VII

Look at the ruined chapel again
    Half-way up in the Alpine gorge!
Is that a tower, I point you plain,
    Or is it a mill, or an iron-forge
Breaks solitude in vain?

VIII

A turn, and we stand in the heart of things;
    The woods are round us, heaped and dim;
From slab to slab how it slips and springs,
    The thread of water single and slim,
Through the ravage some torrent brings!   40

IX

Does it feed the little lake below?
   That speck of white just on its marge
Is Pella; see, in the evening-glow,
   How sharp the silver spear-heads charge
When Alp meets heaven in snow!

X

On our other side is the straight-up rock;
   And a path is kept 'twixt the gorge and it
By boulder-stones where lichens mock
   The marks on a moth, and small ferns fit
Their teeth to the polished block.   50

XI

Oh the sense of the yellow mountain-flowers,
   And thorny balls, each three in one,
The chestnuts throw on our path in showers!
   For the drop of the woodland fruit's begun,
These early November hours,

XII

That crimson the creeper's leaf across
   Like a splash of blood, intense, abrupt,
O'er a shield else gold from rim to boss,
   And lay it for show on the fairy-cupped
Elf-needled mat of moss,   60

XIII

By the rose-flesh mushrooms, undivulged
   Last evening – nay, in today's first dew
Yon sudden coral nipple bulged,
   Where a freaked fawn-coloured flaky crew
Of toadstools peep indulged.

And yonder, at foot of the fronting ridge
    That takes the turn to a range beyond,
Is the chapel reached by the one-arched bridge
    Where the water is stopped in a stagnant pond
Danced over by the midge.   70

XV

The chapel and bridge are of stone alike,
    Blackish-grey and mostly wet;
Cut hemp-stalks steep in the narrow dyke.
    See here again, how the lichens fret
And the roots of the ivy strike!

XVI

Poor little place, where its one priest comes
    On a festa-day, if he comes at all,
To the dozen folk from their scattered homes,
    Gathered within that precinct small
By the dozen ways one roams –   80

XVII

To drop from the charcoal-burners' huts,
    Or climb from the hemp-dressers' low shed,
Leave the grange where the woodman stores his nuts,
    Or the wattled cote where the fowlers spread
Their gear on the rock's bare juts.

XVIII

It has some pretension too, this front,
    With its bit of fresco half-moon-wise
Set over the porch, Art's early wont:
    'Tis John in the Desert, I surmise,
But has borne the weather's brunt –   90

XIX

Not from the fault of the builder, though,
  For a pent-house properly projects
Where three carved beams make a certain show,
  Dating – good thought of our architect's –
'Five, six, nine, he lets you know.

XX

And all day long a bird sings there,
  And a stray sheep drinks at the pond at times;
The place is silent and aware;
  It has had its scenes, its joys and crimes,
But that is its own affair.   100

XXI

My perfect wife, my Leonor,
  Oh heart, my own, oh eyes, mine too,
Whom else could I dare look backward for,
  With whom beside should I dare pursue
The path grey heads abhor?

XXII

For it leads to a crag's sheer edge with them;
  Youth, flowery all the way, there stops –
Not they; age threatens and they contemn,
  Till they reach the gulf wherein youth drops,
One inch from life's safe hem!   110

XXIII

With me, youth led . . . I will speak now,
  No longer watch you as you sit
Reading by fire-light, that great brow
  And the spirit-small hand propping it,
Mutely, my heart knows how –

XXIV

When, if I think but deep enough,
    You are wont to answer, prompt as rhyme;
And you, too, find without rebuff
    Response your soul seeks many a time
Piercing its fine flesh-stuff.   120

XXV

My own, confirm me! If I tread
    This path back, is it not in pride
To think how little I dreamed it led
    To an age so blest that, by its side,
Youth seems the waste instead?

XXVI

My own, see where the years conduct!
    At first, 'twas something our two souls
Should mix as mists do; each is sucked
    In each now: on, the new stream rolls,
Whatever rocks obstruct.   130

XXVII

Think, when our one soul understands
    The great Word which makes all things new,
When earth breaks up and heaven expands,
    How will the change strike me and you
In the house not made with hands?

XXVIII

Oh I must feel your brain prompt mine,
    Your heart anticipate my heart,
You must be just before, in fine,
    See and make me see, for your part,
New depths of the divine!   140

XXIX

But who could have expected this
    When we two drew together first
Just for the obvious human bliss,
    To satisfy life's daily thirst
With a thing men seldom miss?

XXX

Come back with me to the first of all,
    Let us lean and love it over again,
Let us now forget and now recall,
    Break the rosary in a pearly rain,
And gather what we let fall!   150

XXXI

What did I say? – that a small bird sings
    All day long, save when a brown pair
Of hawks from the wood float with wide wings
    Strained to a bell: 'gainst noon-day glare
You count the streaks and rings.

XXXII

But at afternoon or almost eve
    'Tis better; then the silence grows
To that degree, you half believe
    It must get rid of what it knows,
Its bosom does so heave.   160

XXXIII

Hither we walked then, side by side,
    Arm in arm and cheek to cheek,
And still I questioned or replied,
    While my heart, convulsed to really speak,
Lay choking in its pride.

XXXIV

Silent the crumbling bridge we cross,
   And pity and praise the chapel sweet,
And care about the fresco's loss,
   And wish for our souls a like retreat,
And wonder at the moss.   170

XXXV

Stoop and kneel on the settle under,
   Look through the window's grated square:
Nothing to see! For fear of plunder,
   The cross is down and the altar bare,
As if thieves don't fear thunder.

XXXVI

We stoop and look in through the grate,
   See the little porch and rustic door,
Read duly the dead builder's date;
   Then cross the bridge that we crossed before,
Take the path again – but wait!   180

XXXVII

Oh moment, one and infinite!
   The water slips o'er stock and stone;
The West is tender, hardly bright:
   How grey at once is the evening grown –
One star, its chrysolite!

XXXVIII

We two stood there with never a third,
   But each by each, as each knew well:
The sights we saw and the sounds we heard,
   The lights and the shades made up a spell
Till the trouble grew and stirred.   190

Oh, the little more, and how much it is!
   And the little less, and what worlds away!
How a sound shall quicken content to bliss,
   Or a breath suspend the blood's best play,
And life be a proof of this!

Had she willed it, still had stood the screen
   So slight, so sure, 'twixt my love and her:
I could fix her face with a guard between,
   And find her soul as when friends confer,
Friends – lovers that might have been.   200

For my heart had a touch of the woodland-time,
   Wanting to sleep now over its best.
Shake the whole tree in the summer-prime,
   But bring to the last leaf no such test!
'Hold the last fast!' runs the rhyme.

For a chance to make your little much,
   To gain a lover and lose a friend,
Venture the tree and a myriad such,
   When nothing you mar but the year can mend:
But a last leaf – fear to touch!   210

Yet should it unfasten itself and fall
   Eddying down till it find your face
At some slight wind – best chance of all!
   Be your heart henceforth its dwelling-place
You trembled to forestall!

XLIV

Worth how well, those dark grey eyes,
    That hair so dark and dear, how worth
That a man should strive and agonize,
    And taste a veriest hell on earth
For the hope of such a prize!   220

XLV

You might have turned and tried a man,
    Set him a space to weary and wear,
And prove which suited more your plan,
    His best of hope or his worst despair,
Yet end as he began.

XLVI

But you spared me this, like the heart you are,
    And filled my empty heart at a word.
If two lives join, there is oft a scar,
    They are one and one, with a shadowy third;
One near one is too far.   230

XLVII

A moment after, and hands unseen
    Were hanging the night around us fast;
But we knew that a bar was broken between
    Life and life: we were mixed at last
In spite of the mortal screen.

XLVIII

The forests had done it; there they stood;
    We caught for a moment the powers at play:
They had mingled us so, for once and good,
    Their work was done – we might go or stay,
They relapsed to their ancient mood.   240

XLIX

How the world is made for each of us!
    How all we perceive and know in it
Tends to some moment's product thus,
    When a soul declares itself – to wit,
By its fruit, the thing it does!

L

Be hate that fruit or love that fruit,
    It forwards the general deed of man,
And each of the Many helps to recruit
    The life of the race by a general plan;
Each living his own, to boot.   250

LI

I am named and known by that moment's feat;
    There took my station and degree;
So grew my own small life complete,
    As nature obtained her best of me –
One born to love you, sweet!

LII

And to watch you sink by the fire-side now
    Back again, as you mutely sit
Musing by fire-light, that great brow
    And the spirit-small hand propping it,
Yonder, my heart knows how!   260

LIII

So, earth has gained by one man the more,
    And the gain of earth must be heaven's gain too;
And the whole is well worth thinking o'er
    When autumn comes: which I mean to do
One day, as I said before.

AN EPISTLE

Containing the strange medical experience of Karshish,
the Arab physician

Karshish, the picker-up of learning's crumbs,
The not-incurious in God's handiwork
(This man's-flesh he hath admirably made,
Blown like a bubble, kneaded like a paste,
To coop up and keep down on earth a space
That puff of vapour from his mouth, man's soul)
– To Abib, all-sagacious in our art,
Breeder in me of what poor skill I boast,
Like me inquisitive how pricks and cracks
Befall the flesh through too much stress and strain, 10
Whereby the wily vapour fain would slip
Back and rejoin its source before the term, –
And aptest in contrivance (under God)
To baffle it by deftly stopping such: –
The vagrant Scholar to his Sage at home
Sends greeting (health and knowledge, fame with peace)
Three samples of true snakestone – rarer still,
One of the other sort, the melon-shaped,
(But fitter, pounded fine, for charms than drugs)
And writeth now the twenty-second time. 20

My journeyings were brought to Jericho:
Thus I resume. Who studious in our art
Shall count a little labour unrepaid?
I have shed sweat enough, left flesh and bone
On many a flinty furlong of this land.
Also, the country-side is all on fire
With rumours of a marching hitherward:
Some say Vespasian cometh, some, his son.
A black lynx snarled and pricked a tufted ear;
Lust of my blood inflamed his yellow balls: 30
I cried and threw my staff and he was gone.
Twice have the robbers stripped and beaten me,
And once a town declared me for a spy;
But at the end, I reach Jerusalem,

Since this poor covert where I pass the night,
This Bethany, lies scarce the distance thence
A man with plague-sores at the third degree
Runs till he drops down dead. Thou laughest here!
'Sooth, it elates me, thus reposed and safe,
To void the stuffing of my travel-scrip   40
And share with thee whatever Jewry yields.
A viscid choler is observable
In tertians, I was nearly bold to say;
And falling-sickness hath a happier cure
Than our school wots of: there's a spider here
Weaves no web, watches on the ledge of tombs,
Sprinkled with mottles on an ash-grey back;
Take five and drop them . . . but who knows his mind,
The Syrian runagate I trust this to?
His service payeth me a sublimate   50
Blown up his nose to help the ailing eye.
Best wait: I reach Jerusalem at morn,
There set in order my experiences,
Gather what most deserves, and give thee all –
Or I might add, Judæa's gum-tragacanth
Scales off in purer flakes, shines clearer-grained,
Cracks 'twixt the pestle and the porphyry,
In fine exceeds our produce. Scalp-disease
Confounds me, crossing so with leprosy –
Thou hadst admired one sort I gained at Zoar –   60
But zeal outruns discretion. Here I end.

   Yet stay: my Syrian blinketh gratefully,
Protesteth his devotion is my price –
Suppose I write what harms not, though he steal?
I half resolve to tell thee, yet I blush,
What set me off a-writing first of all.
An itch I had, a sting to write, a tang!
For, be it this town's barrenness – or else
The Man had something in the look of him –
His case has struck me far more than 'tis worth.   70
So, pardon if – (lest presently I lose
In the great press of novelty at hand
The care and pains this somehow stole from me)

I bid thee take the thing while fresh in mind,
Almost in sight – for, wilt thou have the truth?
The very man is gone from me but now,
Whose ailment is the subject of discourse.
Thus then, and let thy better wit help all!

'Tis but a case of mania – subinduced
By epilepsy, at the turning-point
Of trance prolonged unduly some three days:
When, by the exhibition of some drug
Or spell, exorcization, stroke of art
Unknown to me and which 'twere well to know,
The evil thing out-breaking all at once
Left the man whole and sound of body indeed, –
But, flinging (so to speak) life's gates too wide,
Making a clear house of it too suddenly,
The first conceit that entered might inscribe
Whatever it was minded on the wall
So plainly at that vantage, as it were,
(First come, first served) that nothing subsequent
Attaineth to erase those fancy-scrawls
The just-returned and new-established soul
Hath gotten now so thoroughly by heart
That henceforth she will read or these or none.
And first – the man's own firm conviction rests
That he was dead (in fact they buried him)
– That he was dead and then restored to life
By a Nazarene physician of his tribe:
– 'Sayeth, the same bade 'Rise,' and he did rise.
'Such cases are diurnal,' thou wilt cry.
Not so this figment! – not, that such a fume,
Instead of giving way to time and health,
Should eat itself into the life of life,
As saffron tingeth flesh, blood, bones and all!
For see, how he takes up the after-life.
The man – it is one Lazarus a Jew,
Sanguine, proportioned, fifty years of age,
The body's habit wholly laudable,
As much, indeed, beyond the common health
As he were made and put aside to show.

80

90

100

110

Think, could we penetrate by any drug
And bathe the wearied soul and worried flesh,
And bring it clear and fair, by three days' sleep!
Whence has the man the balm that brightens all?
This grown man eyes the world now like a child.
Some elders of his tribe, I should premise,
Led in their friend, obedient as a sheep,
To bear my inquisition. While they spoke,   120
Now sharply, now with sorrow, – told the case, –
He listened not except I spoke to him,
But folded his two hands and let them talk,
Watching the flies that buzzed: and yet no fool.
And that's a sample how his years must go.
Look, if a beggar, in fixed middle-life,
Should find a treasure, – can he use the same
With straitened habits and with tastes starved small,
And take at once to his impoverished brain
The sudden element that changes things,   130
That sets the undreamed-of rapture at his hand
And puts the cheap old joy in the scorned dust?
Is he not such an one as moves to mirth –
Warily parsimonious, when no need,
Wasteful as drunkenness at undue times?
All prudent counsel as to what befits
The golden mean, is lost on such an one:
The man's fantastic will is the man's law.
So here – we call the treasure knowledge, say,
Increased beyond the fleshly faculty –   140
Heaven opened to a soul while yet on earth,
Earth forced on a soul's use while seeing heaven:
The man is witless of the size, the sum,
The value in proportion of all things,
Or whether it be little or be much.
Discourse to him of prodigious armaments
Assembled to besiege his city now,
And of the passing of a mule with gourds –
'Tis one! Then take it on the other side,
Speak of some trifling fact, – he will gaze rapt   150
With stupor at its very littleness,
(Far as I see) as if in that indeed

He caught prodigious import, whole results;
And so will turn to us the bystanders
In ever the same stupor (note this point)
That we too see not with his opened eyes.
Wonder and doubt come wrongly into play,
Preposterously, at cross-purposes.
Should his child sicken unto death, – why, look
For scarce abatement of his cheerfulness,   160
Or pretermission of the daily craft!
While a word, gesture, glance from that same child
At play or in the school or laid asleep,
Will startle him to an agony of fear,
Exasperation, just as like. Demand
The reason why – ''tis but a word,' object –
'A gesture' – he regards thee as our lord
Who lived there in the pyramid alone,
Looked at us (dost thou mind?) when, being young,
We both would unadvisedly recite   170
Some charm's beginning, from that book of his,
Able to bid the sun throb wide and burst
All into stars, as suns grown old are wont.
Thou and the child have each a veil alike
Thrown o'er your heads, from under which ye both
Stretch your blind hands and trifle with a match
Over a mine of Greek fire, did ye know!
He holds on firmly to some thread of life –
(It is the life to lead perforcedly)
Which runs across some vast distracting orb   180
Of glory on either side that meagre thread,
Which, conscious of, he must not enter yet –
The spiritual life around the earthly life:
The law of that is known to him as this,
His heart and brain move there, his feet stay here.
So is the man perplext with impulses
Sudden to start off crosswise, not straight on,
Proclaiming what is right and wrong across,
And not along, this black thread through the blaze –
'It should be' baulked by 'here it cannot be.'   190
And oft the man's soul springs into his face
As if he saw again and heard again

His sage that bade him 'Rise' and he did rise.
Something, a word, a tick o' the blood within
Admonishes: then back he sinks at once
To ashes, who was very fire before,
In sedulous recurrence to his trade
Whereby he earneth him the daily bread;
And studiously the humbler for that pride,
Professedly the faultier that he knows   200
God's secret, while he holds the thread of life.
Indeed the especial marking of the man
Is prone submission to the heavenly will –
Seeing it, what it is, and why it is.
'Sayeth, he will wait patient to the last
For that same death which must restore his being
To equilibrium, body loosening soul
Divorced even now by premature full growth:
He will live, nay, it pleaseth him to live
So long as God please, and just how God please.   210
He even seeketh not to please God more
(Which meaneth, otherwise) than as God please.
Hence, I perceive not he affects to preach
The doctrine of his sect whate'er it be,
Make proselytes as madmen thirst to do:
How can he give his neighbour the real ground,
His own conviction? Ardent as he is –
Call his great truth a lie, why, still the old
'Be it as God please' reassureth him.
I probed the sore as thy disciple should: 220
'How, beast,' said I, 'this stolid carelessness
Sufficeth thee, when Rome is on her march
To stamp out like a little spark thy town,
Thy tribe, thy crazy tale and thee at once?'
He merely looked with his large eyes on me.
The man is apathetic, you deduce?
Contrariwise, he loves both old and young,
Able and weak, affects the very brutes
And birds – how say I? flowers of the field –
As a wise workman recognizes tools   230
In a master's workshop, loving what they make.
Thus is the man as harmless as a lamb:

Only impatient, let him do his best,
At ignorance and carelessness and sin –
An indignation which is promptly curbed:
As when in certain travels I have feigned
To be an ignoramus in our art
According to some preconceived design,
And happed to hear the land's practitioners
Steeped in conceit sublimed by ignorance,   240
Prattle fantastically on disease,
Its cause and cure – and I must hold my peace!

    Thou wilt object – Why have I not ere this
Sought out the sage himself, the Nazarene
Who wrought this cure, inquiring at the source,
Conferring with the frankness that befits?
Alas! it grieveth me, the learned leech
Perished in a tumult many years ago,
Accused, – our learning's fate, – of wizardry,
Rebellion, to the setting up a rule   250
And creed prodigious as described to me.
His death, which happened when the earthquake fell
(Prefiguring, as soon appeared, the loss
To occult learning in our lord the sage
Who lived there in the pyramid alone)
Was wrought by the mad people – that's their wont!
On vain recourse, as I conjecture it,
To his tried virtue, for miraculous help –
How could he stop the earthquake? That's their way!
The other imputations must be lies: 260
But take one, though I loathe to give it thee,
In mere respect for any good man's fame.
(And after all, our patient Lazarus
Is stark mad; should we count on what he says?
Perhaps not: though in writing to a leech
'Tis well to keep back nothing of a case.)
This man so cured regards the curer, then,
As – God forgive me! who but God himself,
Creator and sustainer of the world,
That came and dwelt in flesh on it awhile!   270
– 'Sayeth that such an one was born and lived,

Taught, healed the sick, broke bread at his own house,
Then died, with Lazarus by, for aught I know,
And yet was . . . what I said nor choose repeat,
And must have so avouched himself, in fact,
In hearing of this very Lazarus
Who saith – but why all this of what he saith?
Why write of trivial matters, things of price
Calling at every moment for remark?
I noticed on the margin of a pool   280
Blue-flowering borage, the Aleppo sort,
Aboundeth, very nitrous. It is strange!

   Thy pardon for this long and tedious case,
Which, now that I review it, needs must seem
Unduly dwelt on, prolixly set forth!
Nor I myself discern in what is writ
Good cause for the peculiar interest
And awe indeed this man has touched me with.
Perhaps the journey's end, the weariness
Had wrought upon me first. I met him thus: 290
I crossed a ridge of short sharp broken hills
Like an old lion's cheek teeth. Out there came
A moon made like a face with certain spots
Multiform, manifold and menacing:
Then a wind rose behind me. So we met
In this old sleepy town at unaware,
The man and I. I send thee what is writ.
Regard it as a chance, a matter risked
To this ambiguous Syrian – he may lose,
Or steal, or give it thee with equal good.   300
Jerusalem's repose shall make amends
For time this letter wastes, thy time and mine;
Till when, once more thy pardon and farewell!

   The very God! think, Abib; dost thou think?
So, the All-Great, were the All-Loving too –
So, through the thunder comes a human voice
Saying, 'O heart I made, a heart beats here!
Face, my hands fashioned, see it in myself!
Thou hast no power nor mayst conceive of mine,

But love I gave thee, with myself to love,   310
And thou must love me who have died for thee!'
The madman saith He said so: it is strange.

'CHILDE ROLAND TO THE DARK TOWER CAME'

(See Edgar's song in Lear)

I

My first thought was, he lied in every word,
    That hoary cripple, with malicious eye
    Askance to watch the working of his lie
On mine, and mouth scarce able to afford
Suppression of the glee, that pursed and scored
    Its edge, at one more victim gained thereby.

II

What else should he be set for, with his staff?
    What, save to waylay with his lies, ensnare
    All travellers who might find him posted there,
And ask the road? I guessed what skull-like laugh   10
Would break, what crutch 'gin write my epitaph
    For pastime in the dusty thoroughfare,

III

If at his counsel I should turn aside
    Into that ominous tract which, all agree,
    Hides the Dark Tower. Yet acquiescingly
I did turn as he pointed: neither pride
Nor hope rekindling at the end descried,
    So much as gladness that some end might be.

IV

For, what with my whole world-wide wandering,
    What with my search drawn out through years, my
        hope   20

73

Dwindled into a ghost not fit to cope
With that obstreperous joy success would bring, –
I hardly tried now to rebuke the spring
    My heart made, finding failure in its scope.

                            V

As when a sick man very near to death
    Seems dead indeed, and feels begin and end
    The tears and takes the farewell of each friend,
And hears one bid the other go, draw breath
Freelier outside, ('since all is o'er,' he saith,
    'And the blow fallen no grieving can amend;')   30

                            VI

While some discuss if near the other graves
    Be room enough for this, and when a day
    Suits best for carrying the corpse away,
With care about the banners, scarves and staves:
And still the man hears all, and only craves
    He may not shame such tender love and stay.

                            VII

Thus, I had so long suffered in this quest,
    Heard failure prophesied so oft, been writ
    So many times among 'The Band' – to wit,
The knights who to the Dark Tower's search addressed   40
Their steps – that just to fail as they, seemed best,
    And all the doubt was now – should I be fit?

                            VIII

So, quiet as despair, I turned from him,
    That hateful cripple, out of his highway
    Into the path he pointed. All the day
Had been a dreary one at best, and dim
Was settling to its close, yet shot one grim
    Red leer to see the plain catch its estray.

74

For mark! no sooner was I fairly found
  Pledged to the plain, after a pace or two,   50
  Than, pausing to throw backward a last view
O'er the safe road, 'twas gone; grey plain all round:
Nothing but plain to the horizon's bound.
  I might go on; nought else remained to do.

So, on I went. I think I never saw
  Such starved ignoble nature; nothing throve:
  For flowers – as well expect a cedar grove!
But cockle, spurge, according to their law
Might propagate their kind, with none to awe,
  You'd think; a burr had been a treasure-trove.   60

No! penury, inertness and grimace,
  In some strange sort, were the land's portion. 'See
  Or shut your eyes,' said Nature peevishly,
'It nothing skills: I cannot help my case:
'Tis the Last Judgement's fire must cure this place,
  Calcine its clods and set my prisoners free.'

If there pushed any ragged thistle-stalk
  Above its mates, the head was chopped; the bents
  Were jealous else. What made those holes and rents
In the dock's harsh swarth leaves, bruised as to baulk   70
All hope of greenness? 'tis a brute must walk
  Pashing their life out, with a brute's intents.

XIII

As for the grass, it grew as scant as hair
  In leprosy; thin dry blades pricked the mud

Which underneath looked kneaded up with blood.
One stiff blind horse, his every bone a-stare,
Stood stupefied, however he came there:
    Thrust out past service from the devil's stud!

XIV

Alive? he might be dead for aught I know,
    With that red gaunt and colloped neck a-strain,   80
    And shut eyes underneath the rusty mane;
Seldom went such grotesqueness with such woe;
I never saw a brute I hated so;
    He must be wicked to deserve such pain.

XV

I shut my eyes and turned them on my heart.
    As a man calls for wine before he fights,
    I asked one draught of earlier, happier sights,
Ere fitly I could hope to play my part.
Think first, fight afterwards – the soldier's art:
    One taste of the old time sets all to rights.   90

XVI

Not it! I fancied Cuthbert's reddening face
    Beneath its garniture of curly gold,
    Dear fellow, till I almost felt him fold
An arm in mine to fix me to the place,
That way he used. Alas, one night's disgrace!
    Out went my heart's new fire and left it cold.

XVII

Giles then, the soul of honour – there he stands
    Frank as ten years ago when knighted first.
    What honest man should dare (he said) he durst.
Good – but the scene shifts – faugh! what hangman-hands   100
Pin to his breast a parchment? His own bands
    Read it. Poor traitor, spit upon and curst!

XVIII

Better this present than a past like that;
   Back therefore to my darkening path again!
   No sound, no sight as far as eye could strain.
Will the night send a howlet or a bat?
I asked: when something on the dismal flat
   Came to arrest my thoughts and change their train.

XIX

A sudden little river crossed my path
   As unexpected as a serpent comes.   110
   No sluggish tide congenial to the glooms;
This, as it frothed by, might have been a bath
For the fiend's glowing hoof – to see the wrath
   Of its black eddy bespate with flakes and spumes.

XX

So petty yet so spiteful! All along,
   Low scrubby alders kneeled down over it;
   Drenched willows flung them headlong in a fit
Of mute despair, a suicidal throng:
The river which had done them all the wrong,
   Whate'er that was, rolled by, deterred no whit.   120

XXI

Which, while I forded, – good saints, how I feared
   To set my foot upon a dead man's cheek,
   Each step, or feel the spear I thrust to seek
For hollows, tangled in his hair or beard!
– It may have been a water-rat I speared,
   But, ugh! it sounded like a baby's shriek.

XXII

Glad was I when I reached the other bank.
   Now for a better country. Vain presage!

Who were the strugglers, what war did they wage,
Whose savage trample thus could pad the dank   130
Soil to a plash? Toads in a poisoned tank,
   Or wild cats in a red-hot iron cage –

XXIII

The fight must so have seemed in that fell cirque.
   What penned them there, with all the plain to choose?
   No foot-print leading to that horrid mews,
None out of it. Mad brewage set to work
Their brains, no doubt, like galley-slaves the Turk
   Pits for his pastime, Christians against Jews.

XXIV

And more than that – a furlong on – why, there!
   What bad use was that engine for, that wheel,   140
   Or brake, not wheel – that harrow fit to reel
Men's bodies out like silk? with all the air
Of Tophet's tool, on earth left unaware,
   Or brought to sharpen its rusty teeth of steel.

XXV

Then came a bit of stubbed ground, once a wood,
   Next a marsh, it would seem, and now mere earth
   Desperate and done with; (so a fool finds mirth,
Makes a thing and then mars it, till his mood
Changes and off he goes!) within a rood –
   Bog, clay and rubble, sand and stark black dearth.   150

XXVI

Now blotches rankling, coloured gay and grim,
   Now patches where some leanness of the soil's
   Broke into moss or substances like boils;
Then came some palsied oak, a cleft in him
Like a distorted mouth that splits its rim
   Gaping at death, and dies while it recoils.

And just as far as ever from the end!
   Nought in the distance but the evening, nought
   To point my footstep further! At the thought,
A great black bird, Apollyon's bosom-friend,   160
Sailed past, nor beat his wide wing dragon-penned
   That brushed my cap – perchance the guide I sought.

For, looking up, aware I somehow grew,
   'Spite of the dusk, the plain had given place
   All round to mountains – with such name to grace
Mere ugly heights and heaps now stolen in view.
How thus they had surprised me, – solve it, you!
   How to get from them was no clearer case.

Yet half I seemed to recognize some trick
   Of mischief happened to me, God knows when –   170
   In a bad dream perhaps. Here ended, then,
Progress this way. When, in the very nick
Of giving up, one time more, came a click
   As when a trap shuts – you're inside the den!

Burningly it came on me all at once,
   This was the place! those two hills on the right,
   Crouched like two bulls locked horn in horn in fight;
While to the left, a tall scalped mountain . . . Dunce,
Dotard, a-dozing at the very nonce,
   After a life spent training for the sight!   180

What in the midst lay but the Tower itself?
   The round squat turret, blind as the fool's heart,

Built of brown stone, without a counterpart
In the whole world. The tempest's mocking elf
Points to the shipman thus the unseen shelf
    He strikes on, only when the timbers start.

XXXII

Not see? because of night perhaps? – why, day
    Came back again for that! before it left,
    The dying sunset kindled through a cleft:
The hills, like giants at a hunting, lay,   190
Chin upon hand, to see the game at bay, –
    'Now stab and end the creature – to the heft!'

XXXIII

Not hear? when noise was everywhere! it tolled
    Increasing like a bell. Names in my ears
    Of all the lost adventurers my peers, –
How such a one was strong, and such was bold,
And such was fortunate, yet each of old
    Lost, lost! one moment knelled the woe of years.

XXXIV

There they stood, ranged along the hill-sides, met
    To view the last of me, a living frame   200
    For one more picture! in a sheet of flame
I saw them and I knew them all. And yet
Dauntless the slug-horn to my lips I set,
    And blew. *'Childe Roland to the Dark Tower came.'*

LOVE IN A LIFE

I

Room after room,
I hunt the house through
We inhabit together.
Heart, fear nothing, for, heart, thou shalt find her –

Next time, herself! – not the trouble behind her
Left in the curtain, the couch's perfume!
As she brushed it, the cornice-wreath blossomed anew:
Yon looking-glass gleamed at the wave of her feather.

II

Yet the day wears,
And door succeeds door;   10
I try the fresh fortune –
Range the wide house from the wing to the centre.
Still the same chance! she goes out as I enter.
Spend my whole day in the quest, – who cares?
But 'tis twilight, you see, – with such suites to explore,
Such closets to search, such alcoves to importune!

LIFE IN A LOVE

Escape me?
Never –
Beloved!
While I am I, and you are you,
    So long as the world contains us both,
    Me the loving and you the loth,
While the one eludes, must the other pursue.
My life is a fault at last, I fear:
    It seems too much like a fate, indeed!
    Though I do my best I shall scarce succeed.   10
But what if I fail of my purpose here?
It is but to keep the nerves at strain,
    To dry one's eyes and laugh at a fall,
And, baffled, get up and begin again, –
    So the chace takes up one's life, that's all.
While, look but once from your farthest bound
    At me so deep in the dust and dark,
No sooner the old hope goes to ground
    Than a new one, straight to the self-same mark,
I shape me –   20
Ever
Removed!

THE LAST RIDE TOGETHER

I

I said – Then, dearest, since 'tis so,
Since now at length my fate I know,
Since nothing all my love avails,
Since all, my life seemed meant for, fails,
   Since this was written and needs must be –
My whole heart rises up to bless
Your name in pride and thankfulness!
Take back the hope you gave, – I claim
Only a memory of the same,
– And this beside, if you will not blame,   10
   Your leave for one more last ride with me.

II

My mistress bent that brow of hers;
Those deep dark eyes where pride demurs
When pity would be softening through,
Fixed me a breathing-while or two
   With life or death in the balance: right!
The blood replenished me again;
My last thought was at least not vain:
I and my mistress, side by side
Shall be together, breathe and ride,   20
So, one day more am I deified.
   Who knows but the world may end tonight?

III

Hush! if you saw some western cloud
All billowy-bosomed, over-bowed
By many benedictions – sun's
And moon's and evening-star's at once –
   And so, you, looking and loving best,
Conscious grew, your passion drew
Cloud, sunset, moonrise, star-shine too,
Down on you, near and yet more near,   30

Till flesh must fade for heaven was here! –
Thus leant she and lingered – joy and fear!
   Thus lay she a moment on my breast.

IV

Then we began to ride. My soul
Smoothed itself out, a long-cramped scroll
Freshening and fluttering in the wind.
Past hopes already lay behind.
   What need to strive with a life awry?
Had I said that, had I done this,
So might I gain, so might I miss.   40
Might she have loved me? just as well
She might have hated, who can tell!
Where had I been now if the worst befell?
   And here we are riding, she and I.

V

Fail I alone, in words and deeds?
Why, all men strive and who succeeds?
We rode; it seemed my spirit flew,
Saw other regions, cities new,
   As the world rushed by on either side.
I thought, – All labour, yet no less   50
Bear up beneath their unsuccess.
Look at the end of work, contrast
The petty done, the undone vast,
This present of theirs with the hopeful past!
   I hoped she would love me; here we ride.

VI

What hand and brain went ever paired?
What heart alike conceived and dared?
What act proved all its thought had been?
What will but felt the fleshly screen?
   We ride and I see her bosom heave.
There's many a crown for who can reach.

Ten lines, a statesman's life in each!
The flag stuck on a heap of bones,
A soldier's doing! what atones?
They scratch his name on the Abbey-stones.
    My riding is better, by their leave.

VII

What does it all mean, poet? Well,
Your brains beat into rhythm, you tell
What we felt only; you expressed
You hold things beautiful the best,   70
    And pace them in rhyme so, side by side.
'Tis something, nay 'tis much: but then,
Have you yourself what's best for men?
Are you – poor, sick, old ere your time –
Nearer one whit your own sublime
Than we who never have turned a rhyme?
    Sing, riding's a joy! For me, I ride.

VIII

And you, great sculptor – so, you gave
A score of years to Art, her slave,
And that's your Venus, whence we turn   80
To yonder girl that fords the burn!
    You acquiesce, and shall I repine?
What, man of music, you grown grey
With notes and nothing else to say,
Is this your sole praise from a friend,
'Greatly his opera's strains intend,
But in music we know how fashions end!'
    I gave my youth; but we ride, in fine.

IX

Who knows what's fit for us? Had fate
Proposed bliss here should sublimate   90
My being – had I signed the bond –
Still one must lead some life beyond,

Have a bliss to die with, dim-descried.
This foot once planted on the goal,
This glory-garland round my soul,
Could I descry such? Try and test!
I sink back shuddering from the quest.
Earth being so good, would heaven seem best?
　　Now, heaven and she are beyond this ride.

X

And yet – she has not spoke so long! 100
What if heaven be that, fair and strong
At life's best, with our eyes upturned
Whither life's flower is first discerned,
　　We, fixed so, ever should so abide?
What if we still ride on, we two
With life for ever old yet new,
Changed not in kind but in degree,
The instant made eternity, –
And heaven just prove that I and she
　　Ride, ride together, for ever ride? 110

ANDREA DEL SARTO

(Called 'The Faultless Painter')

But do not let us quarrel any more,
No, my Lucrezia; bear with me for once:
Sit down and all shall happen as you wish.
You turn your face, but does it bring your heart?
I'll work then for your friend's friend, never fear,
Treat his own subject after his own way,
Fix his own time, accept too his own price,
And shut the money into this small hand
When next it takes mine. Will it? tenderly?
Oh, I'll content him, – but to-morrow, Love! 10
I often am much wearier than you think,
This evening more than usual, and it seems
As if – forgive now – should you let me sit
Here by the window with your hand in mine

And look a half-hour forth on Fiesole,
Both of one mind, as married people use,
Quietly, quietly the evening through,
I might get up to-morrow to my work
Cheerful and fresh as ever. Let us try.
To-morrow, how you shall be glad for this!   20
Your soft hand is a woman of itself,
And mine the man's bared breast she curls inside.
Don't count the time lost, neither; you must serve
For each of the five pictures we require:
It saves a model. So! keep looking so –
My serpentining beauty, rounds on rounds!
– How could you ever prick those perfect ears,
Even to put the pearl there! oh, so sweet –
My face, my moon, my everybody's moon,
Which everybody looks on and calls his,   30
And, I suppose, is looked on by in turn,
While she looks – no one's: very dear, no less.
You smile? why, there's my picture ready made,
There's what we painters call our harmony!
A common greyness silvers everything, –
All in a twilight, you and I alike
– You, at the point of your first pride in me
(That's gone you know), – but I, at every point;
My youth, my hope, my art, being all toned down
To yonder sober pleasant Fiesole.   40
There's the bell clinking from the chapel-top;
That length of convent-wall across the way
Holds the trees safer, huddled more inside;
The last monk leaves the garden; days decrease,
And autumn grows, autumn in everything.
Eh? the whole seems to fall into a shape
As if I saw alike my work and self
And all that I was born to be and do,
A twilight-piece. Love, we are in God's hand.
How strange now, looks the life he makes us lead;   50
So free we seem, so fettered fast we are!
I feel he laid the fetter: let it lie!
This chamber for example – turn your head –
All that's behind us! You don't understand

Nor care to understand about my art,
But you can hear at least when people speak:
And that cartoon, the second from the door
– It is the thing, Love! so such things should be –
Behold Madonna! – I am bold to say.
I can do with my pencil what I know,   60
What I see, what at bottom of my heart
I wish for, if I ever wish so deep –
Do easily, too – when I say, perfectly,
I do not boast, perhaps: yourself are judge,
Who listened to the Legate's talk last week,
And just as much they used to say in France.
At any rate 'tis easy, all of it!
No sketches first, no studies, that's long past:
I do what many dream of, all their lives,
– Dream? strive to do, and agonize to do,   70
And fail in doing. I could count twenty such
On twice your fingers, and not leave this town,
Who strive – you don't know how the others strive
To paint a little thing like that you smeared
Carelessly passing with your robes afloat, –
Yet do much less, so much less, Someone says,
(I know his name, no matter) – so much less!
Well, less is more, Lucrezia: I am judged.
There burns a truer light of God in them,
In their vexed beating stuffed and stopped-up brain,   80
Heart, or whate'er else, than goes on to prompt
This low-pulsed forthright craftsman's hand of mine.
Their works drop groundward, but themselves, I know,
Reach many a time a heaven that's shut to me,
Enter and take their place there sure enough,
Though they come back and cannot tell the world.
My works are nearer heaven, but I sit here.
The sudden blood of these men! at a word –
Praise them, it boils, or blame them, it boils too.
I, painting from myself and to myself,   90
Know what I do, am unmoved by men's blame
Or their praise either. Somebody remarks
Morello's outline there is wrongly traced,
His hue mistaken; what of that? or else,

Rightly traced and well ordered; what of that?
Speak as they please, what does the mountain care?
Ah, but a man's reach should exceed his grasp,
Or what's a heaven for? All is silver-grey
Placid and perfect with my art: the worse!
I know both what I want and what might gain,   100
And yet how profitless to know, to sigh
'Had I been two, another and myself,
Our head would have o'erlooked the world!' No doubt.
Yonder's a work now, of that famous youth
The Urbinate who died five years ago.
('Tis copied, George Vasari sent it me.)
Well, I can fancy how he did it all,
Pouring his soul, with kings and popes to see,
Reaching, that heaven might so replenish him,
Above and through his art – for it gives way;   110
That arm is wrongly put – and there again –
A fault to pardon in the drawing's lines,
Its body, so to speak: its soul is right,
He means right – that, a child may understand.
Still, what an arm! and I could alter it:
But all the play, the insight and the stretch –
Out of me, out of me! And wherefore out?
Had you enjoined them on me, given me soul,
We might have risen to Rafael, I and you!
Nay, Love, you did give all I asked, I think –   120
More than I merit, yes, by many times.
But had you – oh, with the same perfect brow,
And perfect eyes, and more than perfect mouth,
And the low voice my soul hears, as a bird
The fowler's pipe, and follows to the snare –
Had you, with these the same, but brought a mind!
Some women do so. Had the mouth there urged
'God and the glory! never care for gain.
The present by the future, what is that?
Live for fame, side by side with Agnolo!   130
Rafael is waiting: up to God, all three!'
I might have done it for you. So it seems:
Perhaps not. All is as God over-rules.
Beside, incentives come from the soul's self;

The rest avail not. Why do I need you?
What wife had Rafael, or has Agnolo?
In this world, who can do a thing, will not;
And who would do it, cannot, I perceive:
Yet the will's somewhat – somewhat, too, the power –
And thus we half-men struggle. At the end,   140
God, I conclude, compensates, punishes.
'Tis safer for me, if the award be strict,
That I am something underrated here,
Poor this long while, despised, to speak the truth.
I dared not, do you know, leave home all day,
For fear of chancing on the Paris lords.
The best is when they pass and look aside;
But they speak sometimes; I must bear it all.
Well may they speak! That Francis, that first time,
And that long festal year at Fontainebleau!   150
I surely then could sometimes leave the ground,
Put on the glory, Rafael's daily wear,
In that humane great monarch's golden look, –
One finger in his beard or twisted curl
Over his mouth's good mark that made the smile,
One arm about my shoulder, round my neck,
The jingle of his gold chain in my ear,
I painting proudly with his breath on me,
All his court round him, seeing with his eyes,
Such frank French eyes, and such a fire of souls   160
Profuse, my hand kept plying by those hearts, –
And, best of all, this, this, this face beyond,
This in the background, waiting on my work,
To crown the issue with a last reward!
A good time, was it not, my kingly days?
And had you not grown restless . . . but I know –
'Tis done and past; 'twas right, my instinct said;
Too live the life grew, golden and not grey,
And I'm the weak-eyed bat no sun should tempt
Out of the grange whose four walls make his world.   170
How could it end in any other way?
You called me, and I came home to your heart.
The triumph was – to reach and stay there; since
I reached it ere the triumph, what is lost?

Let my hands frame your face in your hair's gold,
You beautiful Lucrezia that are mine!
'Rafael did this, Andrea painted that;
The Roman's is the better when you pray,
But still the other's Virgin was his wife –'
Men will excuse me. I am glad to judge   180
Both pictures in your presence; clearer grows
My better fortune, I resolve to think.
For, do you know, Lucrezia, as God lives,
Said one day Agnolo, his very self,
To Rafael . . . I have known it all these years . . .
(When the young man was flaming out his thoughts
Upon a palace-wall for Rome to see,
Too lifted up in heart because of it)
'Friend, there's a certain sorry little scrub
Goes up and down our Florence, none cares how,   190
Who, were he set to plan and execute
As you are, pricked on by your popes and kings,
Would bring the sweat into that brow of yours!'
To Rafael's! – And indeed the arm is wrong.
I hardly dare . . . yet, only you to see,
Give the chalk here – quick, thus the line should go!
Ay, but the soul! he's Rafael! rub it out!
Still, all I care for, if he spoke the truth,
(What he? why, who but Michel Agnolo?
Do you forget already words like those?)   200
If really there was such a chance, so lost, –
Is, whether you're – not grateful – but more pleased.
Well, let me think so. And you smile indeed!
This hour has been an hour! Another smile?
If you would sit thus by me every night
I should work better, do you comprehend?
I mean that I should earn more, give you more.
See, it is settled dusk now; there's a star;
Morello's gone, the watch-lights show the wall,
The cue-owls speak the name we call them by.   210
Come from the window, love, – come in, at last,
Inside the melancholy little house
We built to be so gay with. God is just.
King Francis may forgive me: oft at nights

When I look up from painting, eyes tired out,
The walls become illumined, brick from brick
Distinct, instead of mortar, fierce bright gold,
That gold of his I did cement them with!
Let us but love each other. Must you go?
That Cousin here again? he waits outside?   220
Must see you – you, and not with me? Those loans?
More gaming debts to pay? you smiled for that?
Well, let smiles buy me! have you more to spend?
While hand and eye and something of a heart
Are left me, work's my ware, and what's it worth?
I'll pay my fancy. Only let me sit
The grey remainder of the evening out,
Idle, you call it, and muse perfectly
How I could paint, were I but back in France,
One picture, just one more – the Virgin's face,   230
Not yours this time! I want you at my side
To hear them – that is, Michel Agnolo –
Judge all I do and tell you of its worth.
Will you? To-morrow, satisfy your friend.
I take the subjects for his corridor,
Finish the portrait out of hand – there, there,
And throw him in another thing or two
If he demurs; the whole should prove enough
To pay for this same Cousin's freak. Beside,
What's better and what's all I care about,   240
Get you the thirteen scudi for the ruff!
Love, does that please you? Ah, but what does he,
The Cousin! what does he to please you more?

    I am grown peaceful as old age to-night.
I regret little, I would change still less.
Since there my past life lies, why alter it?
The very wrong to Francis! – it is true
I took his coin, was tempted and complied,
And built this house and sinned, and all is said.
My father and my mother died of want.   250
Well, had I riches of my own? you see
How one gets rich! Let each one bear his lot.
They were born poor, lived poor, and poor they died:

And I have laboured somewhat in my time
And not been paid profusely. Some good son
Paint my two hundred pictures – let him try!
No doubt, there's something strikes a balance. Yes,
You loved me quite enough, it seems to-night.
This must suffice me here. What would one have?
In heaven, perhaps, new chances, one more chance –   260
Four great walls in the New Jerusalem,
Meted on each side by the angel's reed,
For Leonard, Rafael, Agnolo and me
To cover – the three first without a wife,
While I have mine! So – still they overcome
Because there's still Lucrezia, – as I choose.

Again the Cousin's whistle! Go, my Love.

CLEON

'As certain also of your own poets have said' –

Cleon the poet (from the sprinkled isles,
Lily on lily, that o'erlace the sea,
And laugh their pride when the light wave lisps 'Greece') –
To Protus in his Tyranny: much health!

    They give thy letter to me, even now:
I read and seem as if I heard thee speak.
The master of thy galley still unlades
Gift after gift; they block my court at last
And pile themselves along its portico
Royal with sunset, like a thought of thee: 10
And one white she-slave from the group dispersed
Of black and white slaves (like the chequer-work
Pavement, at once my nation's work and gift,
Now covered with this settle-down of doves),
One lyric woman, in her crocus vest
Woven of sea-wools, with her two white hands
Commends to me the strainer and the cup
Thy lip hath bettered ere it blesses mine.

Well-counselled, king, in thy munificence!
For so shall men remark, in such an act   20
Of love for him whose song gives life its joy,
Thy recognition of the use of life;
Nor call thy spirit barely adequate
To help on life in straight ways, broad enough
For vulgar souls, by ruling and the rest.
Thou, in the daily building of thy tower, –
Whether in fierce and sudden spasms of toil,
Or through dim lulls of unapparent growth,
Or when the general work 'mid good acclaim
Climbed with the eye to cheer the architect, –   30
Didst ne'er engage in work for mere work's sake –
Hadst ever in thy heart the luring hope
Of some eventual rest a-top of it,
Whence, all the tumult of the building hushed,
Thou first of men mightst look out to the East:
The vulgar saw thy tower, thou sawest the sun.
For this, I promise on thy festival
To pour libation, looking o'er the sea,
Making this slave narrate thy fortunes, speak
Thy great words, and describe thy royal face –   40
Wishing thee wholly where Zeus lives the most,
Within the eventual element of calm.

    Thy letter's first requirement meets me here.
It is as thou hast heard: in one short life
I, Cleon, have effected all those things
Thou wonderingly dost enumerate.
That epos on thy hundred plates of gold
Is mine, – and also mine the little chant,
So sure to rise from every fishing-bark
When, lights at prow, the seamen haul their net.   50
The image of the sun-god on the phare,
Men turn from the sun's self to see, is mine;
The Pœcile, o'er-storied its whole length,
As thou didst hear, with painting, is mine too.
I know the true proportions of a man
And woman also, not observed before;
And I have written three books on the soul,

Proving absurd all written hitherto,
And putting us to ignorance again.
For music, – why, I have combined the moods,   60
Inventing one. In brief, all arts are mine;
Thus much the people know and recognize,
Throughout our seventeen islands. Marvel not.
We of these latter days, with greater mind
Than our forerunners, since more composite,
Look not so great, beside their simple way,
To a judge who only sees one way at once,
One mind-point and no other at a time, –
Compares the small part of a man of us
With some whole man of the heroic age,   70
Great in his way – not ours, nor meant for ours.
And ours is greater, had we skill to know:
For, what we call this life of men on earth,
This sequence of the soul's achievements here
Being, as I find much reason to conceive,
Intended to be viewed eventually
As a great whole, not analyzed to parts,
But each part having reference to all, –
How shall a certain part, pronounced complete,
Endure effacement by another part?   80
Was the thing done? – then, what's to do again?
See, in the chequered pavement opposite,
Suppose the artist made a perfect rhomb,
And next a lozenge, then a trapezoid –
He did not overlay them, superimpose
The new upon the old and blot it out,
But laid them on a level in his work,
Making at last a picture; there it lies.
So, first the perfect separate forms were made,
The portions of mankind; and after, so,   90
Occurred the combination of the same.
For where had been a progress, otherwise?
Mankind, made up of all the single men, –
In such a synthesis the labour ends.
Now mark me! those divine men of old time
Have reached, thou sayest well, each at one point
The outside verge that rounds our faculty;

And where they reached, who can do more than reach?
It takes but little water just to touch
At some one point the inside of a sphere,   100
And, as we turn the sphere, touch all the rest
In due succession: but the finer air
Which not so palpably nor obviously,
Though no less universally, can touch
The whole circumference of that emptied sphere,
Fills it more fully than the water did;
Holds thrice the weight of water in itself
Resolved into a subtler element.
And yet the vulgar call the sphere first full
Up to the visible height – and after, void;   110
Not knowing air's more hidden properties.
And thus our soul, misknown, cries out to Zeus
To vindicate his purpose in our life:
Why stay we on the earth unless to grow?
Long since, I imaged, wrote the fiction out,
That he or other god descended here
And, once for all, showed simultaneously
What, in its nature, never can be shown,
Piecemeal or in succession; – showed, I say,
The worth both absolute and relative   120
Of all his children from the birth of time,
His instruments for all appointed work.
I now go on to image, – might we hear
The judgement which should give the due to each,
Show where the labour lay and where the ease,
And prove Zeus' self, the latent everywhere!
This is a dream: – but no dream, let us hope,
That years and days, the summers and the springs,
Follow each other with unwaning powers.
The grapes which dye thy wine are richer far,   130
Through culture, than the wild wealth of the rock;
The suave plum than the savage-tasted drupe;
The pastured honey-bee drops choicer sweet;
The flowers turn double, and the leaves turn flowers;
That young and tender crescent-moon, thy slave,
Sleeping above her robe as buoyed by clouds,
Refines upon the women of my youth.

What, and the soul alone deteriorates?
I have not chanted verse like Homer, no –
Nor swept string like Terpander, no – nor carved   140
And painted men like Phidias and his friend:
I am not great as they are, point by point.
But I have entered into sympathy
With these four, running these into one soul,
Who, separate, ignored each other's art.
Say, is it nothing that I know them all?
The wild flower was the larger; I have dashed
Rose-blood upon its petals, pricked its cup's
Honey with wine, and driven its seed to fruit,
And show a better flower if not so large: 150
I stand myself. Refer this to the gods
Whose gift alone it is! which, shall I dare
(All pride apart) upon the absurd pretext
That such a gift by chance lay in my hand,
Discourse of lightly or depreciate?
It might have fallen to another's hand: what then?
I pass too surely: let at least truth stay!

     And next, of what thou followest on to ask.
This being with me as I declare, O king,
My works, in all these varicoloured kinds,   160
So done by me, accepted so by men –
Thou askest, if (my soul thus in men's hearts)
I must not be accounted to attain
The very crown and proper end of life?
Inquiring thence how, now life closeth up,
I face death with success in my right hand:
Whether I fear death less than dost thyself
The fortunate of men? 'For' (writest thou)
'Thou leavest much behind, while I leave nought.
Thy life stays in the poems men shall sing,   170
The pictures men shall study; while my life,
Complete and whole now in its power and joy,
Dies altogether with my brain and arm,
Is lost indeed; since, what survives myself?
The brazen statue to o'erlook my grave,
Set on the promontory which I named.

And that – some supple courtier of my heir
Shall use its robed and sceptred arm, perhaps,
To fix the rope to, which best drags it down,
I go then: triumph thou, who dost not go!'   180

    Nay, thou art worthy of hearing my whole mind.
Is this apparent, when thou turn'st to muse
Upon the scheme of earth and man in chief,
That admiration grows as knowledge grows?
That imperfection means perfection hid,
Reserved in part, to grace the after-time?
If, in the morning of philosophy,
Ere aught had been recorded, nay perceived,
Thou, with the light now in thee, couldst have looked
On all earth's tenantry, from worm to bird,   190
Ere man, her last, appeared upon the stage –
Thou wouldst have seen them perfect, and deduced
The perfectness of others yet unseen.
Conceding which, – had Zeus then questioned thee
'Shall I go on a step, improve on this,
Do more for visible creatures than is done?'
Thou wouldst have answered, 'Ay, by making each
Grow conscious in himself – by that alone.
All's perfect else: the shell sucks fast the rock,
The fish strikes through the sea, the snake both swims   200
And slides, forth range the beasts, the birds take flight,
Till life's mechanics can no further go –
And all this joy in natural life is put
Like fire from off thy finger into each,
So exquisitely perfect is the same.
But 'tis pure fire, and they mere matter are;
It has them, not they it: and so I choose
For man, thy last premeditated work
(If I might add a glory to the scheme)
That a third thing should stand apart from both,   210
A quality arise within his soul,
Which, intro-active, made to supervise
And feel the force it has, may view itself,
And so be happy.' Man might live at first
The animal life: but is there nothing more?

In due time, let him critically learn
How he lives; and, the more he gets to know
Of his own life's adaptabilities,
The more joy-giving will his life become.
Thus man, who hath this quality, is best.   220

    But thou, king, hadst more reasonably said:
'Let progress end at once, – man make no step
Beyond the natural man, the better beast,
Using his senses, not the sense of sense.'
In man there's failure, only since he left
The lower and inconscious forms of life.
We called it an advance, the rendering plain
Man's spirit might grow conscious of man's life,
And, by new lore so added to the old,
Take each step higher over the brute's head.   230
This grew the only life, the pleasure-house,
Watch-tower and treasure-fortress of the soul,
Which whole surrounding flats of natural life
Seemed only fit to yield subsistence to;
A tower that crowns a country. But alas,
The soul now climbs it just to perish there!
For thence we have discovered ('tis no dream –
We know this, which we had not else perceived)
That there's a world of capability
For joy, spread round about us, meant for us,   240
Inviting us; and still the soul craves all,
And still the flesh replies, 'Take no jot more
Than ere thou clombst the tower to look abroad!
Nay, so much less as that fatigue has brought
Deduction to it.' We struggle, fain to enlarge
Our bounded physical recipiency,
Increase our power, supply fresh oil to life,
Repair the waste of age and sickness: no,
It skills not! life's inadequate to joy,
As the soul sees joy, tempting life to take.   250
They praise a fountain in my garden here
Wherein a Naiad sends the water-bow
Thin from her tube; she smiles to see it rise.
What if I told her, it is just a thread

98

From that great river which the hills shut up,
And mock her with my leave to take the same?
The artificer has given her one small tube
Past power to widen or exchange – what boots
To know she might spout oceans if she could?
She cannot lift beyond her first thin thread: 260
And so a man can use but a man's joy
While he sees God's. Is it for Zeus to boast,
'See, man, how happy I live, and despair –
That I may be still happier – for thy use!'
If this were so, we could not thank our lord,
As hearts beat on to doing; 'tis not so –
Malice it is not. Is it carelessness?
Still, no. If care – where is the sign? I ask,
And get no answer, and agree in sum,
O king, with thy profound discouragement,   270
Who seest the wider but to sigh the more.
Most progress is most failure: thou sayest well.

    The last point now: – thou dost except a case –
Holding joy not impossible to one
With artist-gifts – to such a man as I
Who leave behind me living works indeed;
For, such a poem, such a painting lives.
What? dost thou verily trip upon a word,
Confound the accurate view of what joy is
(Caught somewhat clearer by my eyes than thine)   280
With feeling joy? confound the knowing how
And showing how to live (my faculty)
With actually living? – Otherwise
Where is the artist's vantage o'er the king?
Because in my great epos I display
How divers men young, strong, fair, wise, can act –
Is this as though I acted? if I paint,
Carve the young Phoebus, am I therefore young?
Methinks I'm older that I bowed myself
The many years of pain that taught me art!   290
Indeed, to know is something, and to prove
How all this beauty might be enjoyed, is more:
But, knowing nought, to enjoy is something too.

Yon rower, with the moulded muscles there,
Lowering the sail, is nearer it than I.
I can write love-odes: thy fair slave's an ode.
I get to sing of love, when grown too grey
For being beloved: she turns to that young man,
The muscles all a-ripple on his back.
I know the joy of kingship: well, thou art king!   300

　　'But,' sayest thou – (and I marvel, I repeat
To find thee trip on such a mere word) 'what
Thou writest, paintest, stays; that does not die:
Sappho survives, because we sing her songs,
And Æschylus, because we read his plays!'
Why, if they live still, let them come and take
Thy slave in my despite, drink from thy cup,
Speak in my place. Thou diest while I survive?
Say rather that my fate is deadlier still,
In this, that every day my sense of joy   310
Grows more acute, my soul (intensified
By power and insight) more enlarged, more keen;
While every day my hairs fall more and more,
My hand shakes, and the heavy years increase –
The horror quickening still from year to year,
The consummation coming past escape
When I shall know most, and yet least enjoy –
When all my works wherein I prove my worth,
Being present still to mock me in men's mouths,
Alive still, in the praise of such as thou,   320
I, I the feeling, thinking, acting man,
The man who loved his life so over-much,
Sleep in my urn. It is so horrible,
I dare at times imagine to my need
Some future state revealed to us by Zeus,
Unlimited in capability
For joy, as this is in desire for joy,
– To seek which, the joy-hunger forces us:
That, stung by straitness of our life, made strait
On purpose to make prized the life at large –   330
Freed by the throbbing impulse we call death,
We burst there as the worm into the fly,

100

Who, while a worm still, wants his wings. But no!
Zeus has not yet revealed it; and alas,
He must have done so, were it possible!

Live long and happy, and in that thought die:
Glad for what was! Farewell. And for the rest,
I cannot tell thy messenger aright
Where to deliver what he bears of thine
To one called Paulus; we have heard his fame   340
Indeed, if Christus be not one with him –
I know not, nor am troubled much to know.
Thou canst not think a mere barbarian Jew,
As Paulus proves to be, one circumcized,
Hath access to a secret shut from us?
Thou wrongest our philosophy, O king,
In stooping to inquire of such an one,
As if his answer could impose at all!
He writeth, doth he? well, and he may write.
Oh, the Jew findeth scholars! certain slaves   350
Who touched on this same isle, preached him and Christ;
And (as I gathered from a bystander)
Their doctrine could be held by no sane man.

TWO IN THE CAMPAGNA

I

I wonder do you feel to-day
    As I have felt since, hand in hand,
We sat down on the grass, to stray
    In spirit better through the land,
This morn of Rome and May?

II

For me, I touched a thought, I know,
    Has tantalized me many times,
(Like turns of thread the spiders throw
    Mocking across our path) for rhymes
To catch at and let go.   10

101

III

Help me to hold it! First it left
   The yellowing fennel, run to seed
There, branching from the brickwork's cleft,
   Some old tomb's ruin: yonder weed
Took up the floating weft,

IV

Where one small orange cup amassed
   Five beetles, – blind and green they grope
Among the honey-meal: and last,
   Everywhere on the grassy slope
I traced it. Hold it fast!   20

V

The champaign with its endless fleece
   Of feathery grasses everywhere!
Silence and passion, joy and peace,
   An everlasting wash of air –
Rome's ghost since her decease.

VI

Such life here, through such lengths of hours,
   Such miracles performed in play,
Such primal naked forms of flowers,
   Such letting nature have her way
While heaven looks from its towers!   30

VII

How say you? Let us, O my dove,
   Let us be unashamed of soul,
As earth lies bare to heaven above!
   How is it under our control
To love or not to love?

VIII

I would that you were all to me,
    You that are just so much, no more.
Nor yours nor mine, nor slave nor free!
    Where does the fault lie? What the core
O' the wound, since wound must be?   40

IX

I would I could adopt your will,
    See with your eyes, and set my heart
Beating by yours, and drink my fill
    At your soul's springs, – your part my part
In life, for good and ill.

X

No. I yearn upward, touch you close,
    Then stand away. I kiss your cheek,
Catch your soul's warmth, – I pluck the rose
    And love it more than tongue can speak –
Then the good minute goes.   50

XI

Already how am I so far
    Out of that minute? Must I go
Still like the thistle-ball, no bar,
    Onward, whenever light winds blow,
Fixed by no friendly star?

XII

Just when I seemed about to learn!
    Where is the thread now? Off again!
The old trick! Only I discern –
    Infinite passion, and the pain
Of finite hearts that yearn.   60

from
Dramatis Personae (1864)

JAMES LEE'S WIFE

I   James Lee's Wife Speaks at the Window

I

Ah, Love, but a day
   And the world has changed!
The sun's away,
   And the bird estranged;
The wind has dropped,
   And the sky's deranged:
Summer has stopped.

II

Look in my eyes!
   Wilt thou change too?
Should I fear surprise?
   Shall I find aught new
In the old and dear,
   In the good and true,
With the changing year?

III

Thou art a man,
   But I am thy love.
For the lake, its swan;
   For the dell, its dove;
And for thee – (oh, haste!)
   Me, to bend above,   20
Me, to hold embraced.

II   *By the Fireside*

I

Is all our fire of shipwreck wood,
   Oak and pine?
Oh, for the ills half-understood,
   The dim dead woe
   Long ago
Befallen this bitter coast of France!
Well, poor sailors took their chance;
   I take mine.

II

A ruddy shaft our fire must shoot   30
   O'er the sea:
Do sailors eye the casement – mute,
   Drenched and stark,
   From their bark –
And envy, gnash their teeth for hate
O' the warm safe house and happy freight
   – Thee and me?

III

God help you, sailors, at your need!
   Spare the curse!
For some ships, safe in port indeed,   40
   Rot and rust,
   Run to dust,

All through worms i' the wood, which crept,
Gnawed our hearts out while we slept:
    That is worse.

IV

Who lived here before us two?
    Old-world pairs.
Did a woman ever – would I knew! –
    Watch the man
    With whom began   50
Love's voyage full-sail, – (now, gnash your teeth!)
When planks start, open hell beneath
    Unawares?

III   In the Doorway

I

The swallow has set her six young on the rail,
    And looks sea-ward:
The water's in stripes like a snake, olive-pale
    To the leeward, –
On the weather-side, black, spotted white with the wind.
'Good fortune departs, and disaster's behind,' –
Hark, the wind with its wants and its infinite wail!   60

II

Our fig-tree, that leaned for the saltness, has furled
    Her five fingers,
Each leaf like a hand opened wide to the world
    Where there lingers
No glint of the gold, Summer sent for her sake:
How the vines writhe in rows, each impaled on its stake!
My heart shrivels up and my spirit shrinks curled.

III

Yet here are we two; we have love, house enough,
    With the field there,

106

This house of four rooms, that field red and rough,   70
   Though it yield there,
For the rabbit that robs, scarce a blade or a bent;
If a magpie alight now, it seems an event;
And they both will be gone at November's rebuff.

IV

But why must cold spread? but wherefore bring change
   To the spirit,
God meant should mate his with an infinite range,
   And inherit
His power to put life in the darkness and cold?
Oh, live and love worthily, bear and be bold!   80
Whom Summer made friends of, let Winter estrange!

IV   Along the Beach

I

I will be quiet and talk with you,
   And reason why you are wrong.
You wanted my love – is that much true?
And so I did love, so I do:
   What has come of it all along?

II

I took you – how could I otherwise?
   For a world to me, and more;
For all, love greatens and glorifies
Till God's a-glow, to the loving eyes,   90
   In what was mere earth before.

III

Yes, earth – yes, mere ignoble earth!
   Now do I mis-state, mistake?
Do I wrong your weakness and call it worth?
Expect all harvest, dread no dearth,
   Seal my sense up for your sake?

107

IV

Oh, Love, Love, no, Love! not so, indeed!
   You were just weak earth, I knew:
With much in you waste, with many a weed,
And plenty of passions run to seed,   100
   But a little good grain too.

V

And such as you were, I took you for mine:
   Did not you find me yours,
To watch the olive and wait the vine,
And wonder when rivers of oil and wine
   Would flow, as the Book assures?

VI

Well, and if none of these good things came,
   What did the failure prove?
The man was my whole world, all the same,
With his flowers to praise or his weeds to blame,   110
   And, either or both, to love.

VII

Yet this turns now to a fault – there! there!
   That I do love, watch too long,
And wait too well, and weary and wear;
And 'tis all an old story, and my despair
   Fit subject for some new song:

VIII

'How the light, light love, he has wings to fly
   At suspicion of a bond:
My wisdom has bidden your pleasure good-bye,
Which will turn up next in a laughing eye,   120
   And why should you look beyond?'

V   On the Cliff

I

I leaned on the turf,
I looked at a rock
Left dry by the surf;
For the turf, to call it grass were to mock:
Dead to the roots, so deep was done
The work of the summer sun.

II

And the rock lay flat
As an anvil's face:
No iron like that!   130
Baked dry; of a weed, of a shell, no trace:
Sunshine outside, but ice at the core,
Death's altar by the lone shore.

III

On the turf, sprang gay
With his films of blue,
No cricket, I'll say,
But a warhorse, barded and chanfroned too,
The gift of a quixote-mage to his knight,
Real fairy, with wings all right.

IV

On the rock, they scorch   140
Like a drop of fire
From a brandished torch,
Fall two red fans of a butterfly:
No turf, no rock: in their ugly stead,
See, wonderful blue and red!

Is it not so
With the minds of men?
The level and low,
The burnt and bare, in themselves; but then
With such a blue and red grace, not theirs, –   150
Love settling unawares!

VI *Reading a Book, Under the Cliff*

I

'Still ailing, Wind? Wilt be appeased or no?
    Which needs the other's office, thou or I?
Dost want to be disburthened of a woe,
    And can, in truth, my voice untie
Its links, and let it go?

II

'Art thou a dumb wronged thing that would be righted,
    Entrusting thus thy cause to me? Forbear!
No tongue can mend such pleadings; faith, requited
    With falsehood, – love, at last aware   160
Of scorn, – hopes, early blighted, –

III

'We have them; but I know not any tone
    So fit as thine to falter forth a sorrow:
Dost think men would go mad without a moan,
    If they knew any way to borrow
A pathos like thy own?

IV

'Which sigh wouldst mock, of all the sighs? The one
    So long escaping from lips starved and blue,
That lasts while on her pallet-bed the nun

110

Stretches her length; her foot comes through   170
The straw she shivers on;

V

'You had not thought she was so tall: and spent,
   Her shrunk lids open, her lean fingers shut
Close, close, their sharp and livid nails indent
   The clammy palm; then all is mute:
That way, the spirit went.

VI

'Or wouldst thou rather that I understand
   Thy will to help me? – like the dog I found
Once, pacing sad this solitary strand,
   Who would not take my food, poor hound,   180
But whined and licked my hand.'

———————

VII

All this, and more, comes from some young man's pride
   Of power to see, – in failure and mistake,
Relinquishment, disgrace, on every side, –
   Merely examples for his sake,
Helps to his path untried:

VIII

Instances he must – simply recognize?
   Oh, more than so! – must, with a learner's zeal,
Make doubly prominent, twice emphasize,
   By added touches that reveal   190
The god in babe's disguise.

IX

Oh, he knows what defeat means, and the rest!
   Himself the undefeated that shall be:

111

Failure, disgrace, he flings them you to test, –
    His triumph, in eternity
Too plainly manifest!

                    X

Whence, judge if he learn forthwith what the wind
    Means in its moaning – by the happy prompt
Instinctive way of youth, I mean; for kind
    Calm years, exacting their accompt   200
Of pain, mature the mind:

                    XI

And some midsummer morning, at the lull
    Just about daybreak, as he looks across
A sparkling foreign country, wonderful
    To the sea's edge for gloom and gloss,
Next minute must annul, –

                    XII

Then, when the wind begins among the vines,
    So low, so low, what shall it say but this?
'Here is the change beginning, here the lines
    Circumscribe beauty, set to bliss   210
The limit time assigns.'

                    XIII

Nothing can be as it has been before;
    Better, so call it, only not the same.
To draw one beauty into our hearts' core,
    And keep it changeless! such our claim;
So answered, – Never more!

                    XIV

Simple? Why this is the old woe o' the world;
    Tune, to whose rise and fall we live and die.

112

Rise with it, then! Rejoice that man is hurled
      From change to change unceasingly,
His soul's wings never furled!

XV

That's a new question; still replies the fact,
      Nothing endures: the wind moans, saying so;
We moan in acquiescence: there's life's pact,
      Perhaps probation – do *I* know?
God does: endure his act!

XVI

Only, for man, how bitter not to grave
      On his soul's hands' palms one fair good wise thing
Just as he grasped it! For himself, death's wave;
      While time first washes – ah, the sting! –
O'er all he'd sink to save.

VII   *Among the Rocks*

I

Oh, good gigantic smile o' the brown old earth,
      This autumn morning! How he sets his bones
To bask i' the sun, and thrusts out knees and feet
For the ripple to run over in its mirth;
      Listening the while, where on the heap of stones
The white breast of the sea-lark twitters sweet.

II

That is the doctrine, simple, ancient, true;
      Such is life's trial, as old earth smiles and knows.
If you loved only what were worth your love,   240
Love were clear gain, and wholly well for you:
      Make the low nature better by your throes!
Give earth yourself, go up for gain above!

I

'As like as a Hand to another Hand!'
   Whoever said that foolish thing,
Could not have studied to understand
   The counsels of God in fashioning,
Out of the infinite love of his heart,
This Hand, whose beauty I praise, apart
From the world of wonder left to praise,   250
   If I tried to learn the other ways
Of love in its skill, or love in its power.
   'As like as a Hand to another Hand':
   Who said that, never took his stand,
Found and followed, like me, an hour,
   The beauty in this, – how free, how fine
To fear, almost, – of the limit-line!
As I looked at this, and learned and drew,
   Drew and learned, and looked again,
While fast the happy minutes flew,   260
   Its beauty mounted into my brain,
   And a fancy seized me; I was fain
To efface my work, begin anew,
Kiss what before I only drew;
Ay, laying the red chalk 'twixt my lips,
   With soul to help if the mere lips failed,
   I kissed all right where the drawing ailed,
Kissed fast the grace that somehow slips
Still from one's soulless finger-tips.

II

'Tis a clay cast, the perfect thing,   270
   From Hand live once, dead long ago:
Princess-like it wears the ring
   To fancy's eye, by which we know
That here at length a master found
   His match, a proud lone soul its mate,
As soaring genius sank to ground,

And pencil could not emulate
The beauty in this, – how free, how fine
To fear almost! – of the limit-line.
Long ago the god, like me   280
The worm, learned, each in our degree:
Looked and loved, learned and drew,
    Drew and learned and loved again,
While fast the happy minutes flew,
    Till beauty mounted into his brain
And on the finger which outvied
    His art he placed the ring that's there,
Still by fancy's eye descried,
    In token of a marriage rare:
    For him on earth, his art's despair,   290
For him in heaven, his soul's fit bride.

                        III

Little girl with the poor coarse hand
    I turned from to a cold clay cast –
I have my lesson, understand
    The worth of flesh and blood at last.
Nothing but beauty in a Hand?
    Because he could not change the hue,
    Mend the lines and make them true
To this which met his soul's demand, –
    Would Da Vinci turn from you?   300
I hear him laugh my woes to scorn –
'The fool forsooth is all forlorn
Because the beauty, she thinks best,
Lived long ago or was never born, –
Because no beauty bears the test
In this rough peasant Hand! Confessed!
"Art is null and study void!"
    So sayest thou? So said not I,
    Who threw the faulty pencil by,
And years instead of hours employed,   310
Learning the veritable use
    Of flesh and bone and nerve beneath
    Lines and hue of the outer sheath,

                                                        115

If haply I might reproduce
One motive of the powers profuse,
Flesh and bone and nerve that make
   The poorest coarsest human hand
   An object worthy to be scanned
A whole life long for their sole sake.
Shall earth and the cramped moment-space   320
Yield the heavenly crowning grace?
Now the parts and then the whole!
Who art though, with stinted soul
   And stunted body, thus to cry
"I love, – shall that be life's strait dole?
   I must live beloved or die!"
This peasant hand that spins the wool
   And bakes the bread, why lives it on,
   Poor and coarse with beauty gone, –
What use survives the beauty?' Fool!   330

Go, little girl with the poor coarse hand!
I have my lesson, shall understand.

IX   *On Deck*

I

There is nothing to remember in me,
   Nothing I ever said with a grace,
Nothing I did that you care to see,
   Nothing I was that deserves a place
In your mind, now I leave you, set you free.

II

Conceded! In turn, concede to me,
   Such things have been as a mutual flame.
Your soul's locked fast; but, love for a key,   340
   You might let it loose, till I grew the same
In your eyes, as in mine you stand: strange plea!

III

For then, then, what would it matter to me
   That I was the harsh ill-favoured one?
We both should be like as pea and pea;
   It was ever so since the world begun:
So, let me proceed with my reverie.

IV

How strange it were if you had all me,
   As I have all you in my heart and brain,
You, whose least word brought gloom or glee,   350
   Who never lifted the hand in vain –
Will hold mine yet, from over the sea!

V

Strange, if a face, when you thought of me,
   Rose like your own face present now,
With eyes as dear in their due degree,
   Much such a mouth, and as bright a brow,
Till you saw yourself, while you cried ' 'Tis She!'

VI

Well, you may, you must, set down to me
   Love that was life, life that was love;
A tenure of breath at your lips' decree,   360
   A passion to stand as your thoughts approve,
A rapture to fall where your foot might be.

VII

But did one touch of such love for me
   Come in a word or a look of yours,
Whose words and looks will, circling, flee
   Round me and round while life endures, –
Could I fancy 'As I feel, thus feels he';

Why, fade you might to a thing like me,
    And your hair grow these coarse hanks of hair,
Your skin, this bark of a gnarled tree, –   370
    You might turn myself! – should I know or care
When I should be dead of joy, James Lee?

ABT VOGLER

*(After he has been extemporizing upon the musical
instrument of his invention)*

I

Would that the structure brave, the manifold music I
      build,
    Bidding my organ obey, calling its keys to their work,
Claiming each slave of the sound, at a touch, as when
      Solomon willed
    Armies of angels that soar, legions of demons that lurk,
Man, brute, reptile, fly, – alien of end and of aim,
    Adverse, each from the other heaven-high, hell-deep
      removed, –
Should rush into sight at once as he named the ineffable
      Name,
    And pile him a palace straight, to pleasure the princess
      he loved!

II

Would it might tarry like his, the beautiful building of
      mine,
    This which my keys in a crowd pressed and importuned
      to raise!   10
Ah, one and all, how they helped, would dispart now and
      now combine,
    Zealous to hasten the work, heighten their master his
      praise!
And one would bury his brow with a blind plunge down
      to hell,

Burrow awhile and build, broad on the roots of things,
Then up again swim into sight, having based me my palace
    well,
  Founded it, fearless of flame, flat on the nether springs.

III

And another would mount and march, like the excellent
    minion he was,
  Ay, another and yet another, one crowd but with many
    a crest,
Raising my rampired walls of gold as transparent as glass,
  Eager to do and die, yield each his place to the rest: 20
For higher still and higher (as a runner tips with fire,
  When a great illumination surprises a festal night –
Outlining round and round Rome's dome from space to
    spire)
  Up, the pinnacled glory reached, and the pride of my
    soul was in sight.

IV

In sight? Not half! for it seemed, it was certain, to match
    man's birth,
  Nature in turn conceived, obeying an impulse as I;
And the emulous heaven yearned down, made effort to
    reach the earth,
  As the earth had done her best, in my passion, to scale
    the sky:
Novel splendours burst forth, grew familiar and dwelt
    with mine,
  Not a point nor peak but found and fixed its wandering
    star;   30
Meteor-moons, balls of blaze: and they did not pale nor
    pine,
  For earth had attained to heaven, there was no more near
    nor far.

V

Nay more; for there wanted not who walked in the glare
    and glow,
    Presences plain in the place; or, fresh from the
      Protoplast,
Furnished for ages to come, when a kindlier wind should
    blow,
    Lured now to begin and live, in a house to their liking at
      last;
Or else the wonderful Dead who have passed through the
    body and gone,
    But were back once more to breathe in an old world
      worth their new:
What never had been, was now; what was, as it shall be
    anon;
    And what is, – shall I say, matched both? for I was made
      perfect too.   40

VI

All through my keys that gave their sounds to a wish of
    my soul,
    All through my soul that praised as its wish flowed
      visibly forth,
All through music and me! For think, had I painted the
    whole,
    Why, there it had stood, to see, nor the process so
      wonder-worth:
Had I written the same, made verse – still, effect proceeds
    from cause,
    Ye know why the forms are fair, ye hear how the tale is
      told;
It is all triumphant art, but art in obedience to laws,
    Painter and poet are proud in the artist-list enrolled:–

VII

But here is the finger of God, a flash of the will that can,
    Existent behind all laws, that made them and, lo, they
      are!   50

And I know not if, save in this, such gift be allowed to
    man,
  That out of three sounds he frame, not a fourth sound,
    but a star.
Consider it well: each tone of our scale in itself is nought;
  It is everywhere in the world – loud, soft, and all is said:
Give it to me to use! I mix it with two in my thought:
  And, there! Ye have heard and seen: consider and bow
    the head!

VIII

Well, it is gone at last, the palace of music I reared;
  Gone! and the good tears start, the praises that come too
    slow;
For one is assured at first, one scarce can say that he feared,
  That he even gave it a thought, the gone thing was to
    go.   60
Never to be again! But many more of the kind
  As good, nay, better perchance: is this your comfort to
    me?
To me, who must be saved because I cling with my mind
  To the same, same self, same love, same God: ay, what
    was, shall be.

IX

Therefore to whom turn I but to thee, the ineffable Name?
  Builder and maker, thou, of houses not made with
    hands!
What, have fear of change from thee who art ever the
    same?
  Doubt that thy power can fill the heart that thy power
    expands?
There shall never be one lost good! What was, shall live as
    before;
  The evil is null, is nought, is silence implying sound;   70
What was good shall be good, with, for evil, so much
    good more;
  On the earth the broken arcs; in the heaven, a perfect
    round.

All we have willed or hoped or dreamed of good shall
    exist;
  Not its semblance, but itself; no beauty, nor good, nor
    power
Whose voice has gone forth, but each survives for the
    melodist
  When eternity affirms the conception of an hour.
The high that proved too high, the heroic for earth too
    hard,
  The passion that left the ground to lose itself in the sky,
Are music sent up to God by the lover and the bard;
  Enough that he heard it once: we shall hear it by-and-by.   80

XI

And what is our failure here but a triumph's evidence
  For the fulness of the days? Have we withered or
    agonized?
Why else was the pause prolonged but that singing might
    issue thence?
  Why rushed the discords in but that harmony should be
    prized?
Sorrow is hard to bear, and doubt is slow to clear,
  Each sufferer says his say, his scheme of the weal and
    woe:
But God has a few of us whom he whispers in the ear;
  The rest may reason and welcome: 'tis we musicians
    know.

XII

Well, it is earth with me; silence resumes her reign:
  I will be patient and proud, and soberly acquiesce.   90
Give me the keys. I feel for the common chord again,
  Sliding by semitones, till I sink to the minor, – yes,
And I blunt it into a ninth, and I stand on alien ground,
  Surveying awhile the heights I rolled from into the
    deep;

Which, hark, I have dared and done, for my resting-place
    is found,
    The C Major of this life: so, now I will try to sleep.

RABBI BEN EZRA

I

Grow old along with me!
The best is yet to be,
The last of life, for which the first was made:
    Our times are in His hand
    Who saith 'A whole I planned,
Youth shows but half; trust God: see all nor be afraid!'

II

Not that, amassing flowers,
Youth sighed 'Which rose make ours,
Which lily leave and then as best recall?'
    Not that, admiring stars,   10
    It yearned 'Nor Jove, nor Mars;
Mine be some figured flame which blends, transcends
    them all!'

III

Not for such hopes and fears
Annulling youth's brief years,
Do I remonstrate: folly wide the mark!
    Rather I prize the doubt
    Low kinds exist without,
Finished and finite clods, untroubled by a spark.

IV

Poor vaunt of life indeed,
Were man but formed to feed   20
On joy, to solely seek and find and feast:
    Such feasting ended, then

123

As sure an end to men;
Irks care the crop-full bird? Frets doubt the maw-crammed
    beast?

V

Rejoice we are allied
  To That which doth provide
And not partake, effect and not receive!
  A spark disturbs our clod;
  Nearer we hold of God
Who gives, than of His tribes that take, I must believe.   30

VI

Then, welcome each rebuff
  That turns earth's smoothness rough,
Each sting that bids nor sit nor stand but go!
  Be our joys three-parts pain!
  Strive, and hold cheap the strain;
Learn, nor account the pang; dare, never grudge the throe!

VII

For thence, – a paradox
  Which comforts while it mocks, –
Shall life succeed in that it seems to fail:
  What I aspired to be,   40
  And was not, comforts me:
A brute I might have been, but would not sink i' the scale.

VIII

What is he but a brute
  Whose flesh has soul to suit,
Whose spirit works lest arms and legs want play?
  To man, propose this test –
  Thy body at its best,
How far can that project thy soul on its lone way?

124

IX

Yet gifts should prove their use:
   I own the Past profuse   50
Of power each side, perfection every turn:
   Eyes, ears took in their dole,
   Brain treasured up the whole;
Should not the heart beat once 'How good to live and
      learn'?

X

Not once beat 'Praise be Thine!
   I see the whole design,
I, who saw power, see now love perfect too:
   Perfect I call Thy plan:
   Thanks that I was a man!
Maker, remake, complete, – I trust what Thou shalt do!'   60

XI

For pleasant is this flesh;
   Our soul, in its rose-mesh
Pulled ever to the earth, still yearns for rest;
   Would we some prize might hold
   To match those manifold
Possessions of the brute, – gain most, as we did best!

XII

Let us not always say
   'Spite of this flesh to-day
I strove, made head, gained ground upon the whole!'
   As the bird wings and sings,   70
   Let us cry 'All good things
Are ours, nor soul helps flesh more, now, than flesh helps
      soul!'

XIII

Therefore I summon age
   To grant youth's heritage,

125

Life's struggle having so far reached its term:
    Thence shall I pass, approved
    A man, for aye removed
From the developed brute; a god though in the germ.

XIV

    And I shall thereupon
    Take rest, ere I be gone   80
Once more on my adventure brave and new:
    Fearless and unperplexed,
    When I wage battle next,
What weapons to select, what armour to indue.

XV

    Youth ended, I shall try
    My gain or loss thereby;
Leave the fire ashes, what survives is gold:
    And I shall weigh the same,
    Give life its praise or blame:
Young, all lay in dispute; I shall know, being old.   90

XVI

    For note, when evening shuts,
    A certain moment cuts
The deed off, calls the glory from the grey:
    A whisper from the west
    Shoots – 'Add this to the rest,
Take it and try its worth: here dies another day.'

XVII

    So, still within this life,
    Though lifted o'er its strife,
Let me discern, compare, pronounce at last,
    'This rage was right i' the main,   100
    That acquiescence vain:
The Future I may face now I have proved the Past.'

XVIII

For more is not reserved
 To man, with soul just nerved
To act to-morrow what he learns to-day:
    Here, work enough to watch
    The Master work, and catch
Hints of the proper craft, tricks of the tool's true play.

XIX

As it was better, youth
 Should strive, through acts uncouth, 110
Toward making, than repose on aught found made:
    So, better, age, exempt
    From strife, should know, than tempt
Further. Thou waitedest age: wait death nor be afraid!

XX

Enough now, if the Right
 And Good and Infinite
Be named here, as thou callest thy hand thine own,
    With knowledge absolute,
    Subject to no dispute
From fools that crowded youth, nor let thee feel alone. 120

XXI

Be there, for once and all,
 Severed great minds from small,
Announced to each his station in the Past!
    Was I, the world arraigned,
    Were they, my soul disdained,
Right? Let age speak the truth and give us peace at last!

XXII

Now, who shall arbitrate?
 Ten men love what I hate,
Shun what I follow, slight what I receive;

127

Ten, who in ears and eyes   130
    Match me: we all surmise,
They this thing, and I that: whom shall my soul believe?

Not on the vulgar mass
    Called 'work,' must sentence pass,
Things done, that took the eye and had the price;
    O'er which, from level stand,
    The low world laid its hand,
Found straightway to its mind, could value in a trice:

But all, the world's coarse thumb
    And finger failed to plumb,   140
So passed in making up the main account;
    All instincts immature,
    All purposes unsure,
That weighed not as his work, yet swelled the man's
        amount:

Thoughts hardly to be packed
    Into a narrow act,
Fancies that broke through language and escaped;
    All I could never be,
    All, men ignored in me,
This, I was worth to God, whose wheel the pitcher
        shaped.   150

Ay, note that Potter's wheel,
    That metaphor! and feel
Why time spins fast, why passive lies our clay, –
    Thou, to whom fools propound,
    When the wine makes its round,
'Since life fleets, all is change; the Past gone, seize today!'

XXVII

Fool! All that is, at all,
Lasts ever, past recall;
Earth changes, but thy soul and God stand sure:
    What entered into thee,   160
    That was, is, and shall be:
Time's wheel runs back or stops: Potter and clay endure.

XXVIII

He fixed thee mid this dance
Of plastic circumstance,
This Present, thou, forsooth, wouldst fain arrest:
    Machinery just meant
    To give thy soul its bent,
Try thee and turn thee forth, sufficiently impressed.

XXIX

What though the earlier grooves
Which ran the laughing loves   170
Around thy base, no longer pause and press?
    What though, about thy rim,
    Scull-things in order grim
Grow out, in graver mood, obey the sterner stress?

XXX

Look not thou down but up!
To uses of a cup,
The festal board, lamp's flash and trumpet's peal,
    The new wine's foaming flow,
    The Master's lips a-glow!
Thou, heaven's consummate cup, what need'st thou with
    earth's wheel?   180

XXXI

 But I need, now as then,
 Thee, God, who mouldest men;

And since, not even while the whirl was worst,
　　Did I, – to the wheel of life
　　With shapes and colours rife,
Bound dizzily, – mistake my end, to slake Thy thirst:

XXXII

So, take and use Thy work:
　　Amend what flaws may lurk,
What strain o' the stuff, what warpings past the aim!
　　My times be in Thy hand!　　　　　　　　　　　190
　　Perfect the cup as planned!
Let age approve of youth, and death complete the same!

CALIBAN UPON SETEBOS; OR, NATURAL THEOLOGY IN THE
ISLAND

'Thou thoughtest that I was altogether such a one as thyself'

['Will sprawl, now that the heat of day is best,
Flat on his belly in the pit's much mire,
With elbows wide, fists clenched to prop his chin.
And, while he kicks both feet in the cool slush,
And feels about his spine small eft-things course,
Run in and out each arm, and make him laugh:
And while above his head a pompion-plant,
Coating the cave-top as a brow its eye,
Creeps down to touch and tickle hair and beard,
And now a flower drops with a bee inside,　　　　　10
And now a fruit to snap at, catch and crunch, –
He looks out o'er yon sea which sunbeams cross
And recross till they weave a spider-web
(Meshes of fire, some great fish breaks at times)
And talks to his own self, howe'er he please,
Touching that other, whom his dam called God.
Because to talk about Him, vexes – ha,
Could He but know! and time to vex is now,
When talk is safer than in winter-time.
Moreover Prosper and Miranda sleep　　　　　　20
In confidence he drudges at their task,

130

And it is good to cheat the pair, and gibe,
Letting the rank tongue blossom into speech.]

Setebos, Setebos, and Setebos!
'Thinketh, He dwelleth i' the cold o' the moon.

'Thinketh He made it, with the sun to match,
But not the stars; the stars came otherwise;
Only made clouds, winds, meteors, such as that:
Also this isle, what lives and grows thereon,
And snaky sea which rounds and ends the same.   30

'Thinketh, it came of being ill at ease:
He hated that He cannot change His cold,
Nor cure its ache. 'Hath spied an icy fish
That longed to 'scape the rock-stream where she lived,
And thaw herself within the lukewarm brine
O' the lazy sea her stream thrusts far amid,
A crystal spike 'twixt two warm walls of wave;
Only, she ever sickened, found repulse
At the other kind of water, not her life,
(Green-dense and dim-delicious, bred o' the sun)   40
Flounced back from bliss she was not born to breathe,
And in her old bounds buried her despair,
Hating and loving warmth alike: so He.

'Thinketh, He made thereat the sun, this isle,
Trees and the fowls here, beast and creeping thing.
Yon otter, sleek-wet, black, lithe as a leech;
Yon auk, one fire-eye in a ball of foam,
That floats and feeds; a certain badger brown
He hath watched hunt with that slant white-wedge eye
By moonlight; and the pie with the long tongue   50
That pricks deep into oakwarts for a worm,
And says a plain word when she finds her prize,
But will not eat the ants; the ants themselves
That build a wall of seeds and settled stalks
About their hole – He made all these and more,
Made all we see, and us, in spite: how else?
He could not, Himself, make a second self

131

To be His mate; as well have made Himself:
He would not make what he mislikes or slights,
An eyesore to Him, or not worth His pains: 60
But did, in envy, listlessness or sport,
Make what Himself would fain, in a manner, be –
Weaker in most points, stronger in a few,
Worthy, and yet mere playthings all the while,
Things He admires and mocks too, – that is it.
Because, so brave, so better though they be,
It nothing skills if He begin to plague.
Look now, I melt a gourd-fruit into mash,
Add honeycomb and pods, I have perceived,
Which bite like finches when they bill and kiss, –   70
Then, when froth rises bladdery, drink up all,
Quick, quick, till maggots scamper through my brain;
Last, throw me on my back i' the seeded thyme,
And wanton, wishing I were born a bird.
Put case, unable to be what I wish,
I yet could make a live bird out of clay:
Would not I take clay, pinch my Caliban
Able to fly? – for, there, see, he hath wings,
And great comb like the hoopoe's to admire,
And there, a sting to do his foes offence,   80
There, and I will that he begin to live,
Fly to yon rock-top, nip me off the horns
Of grigs high up that make the merry din,
Saucy through their veined wings, and mind me not.
In which feat, if his leg snapped, brittle clay,
And he lay stupid-like, – why, I should laugh;
And if he, spying me, should fall to weep,
Beseech me to be good, repair his wrong,
Bid his poor leg smart less or grow again, –
Well, as the chance were, this might take or else   90
Not take my fancy: I might hear his cry,
And give the mankin three sound legs for one,
Or pluck the other off, leave him like an egg,
And lessoned he was mine and merely clay.
Were this no pleasure, lying in the thyme,
Drinking the mash, with brain become alive,
Making and marring clay at will? So He.

'Thinketh, such shows nor right nor wrong in Him,
Nor kind, nor cruel: He is strong and Lord.
'Am strong myself compared to yonder crabs 100
That march now from the mountain to the sea,
'Let twenty pass, and stone the twenty-first,
Loving not, hating not, just choosing so.
'Say, the first straggler that boasts purple spots
Shall join the file, one pincer twisted off;
'Say, this bruised fellow shall receive a worm,
And two worms he whose nippers end in red;
As it likes me each time, I do: so He.

Well then, 'supposeth He is good i' the main,
Placable if His mind and ways were guessed, 110
But rougher than His handiwork, be sure!
Oh, He hath made things worthier than Himself,
And envieth that, so helped, such things do more
Than He who made them! What consoles but this?
That they, unless through Him, do nought at all,
And must submit: what other use in things?
'Hath cut a pipe of pithless elder-joint
That, blown through, gives exact the scream o' the jay
When from her wing you twitch the feathers blue:
Sound this, and little birds that hate the jay 120
Flock within stone's throw, glad their foe is hurt:
Put case such pipe could prattle and boast forsooth
'I catch the birds, I am the crafty thing,
I make the cry my maker cannot make
With his great round mouth; he must blow through mine!'
Would not I smash it with my foot? So He.

But wherefore rough, why cold and ill at ease?
Aha, that is a question! Ask, for that,
What knows, – the something over Setebos
That made Him, or He, may be, found and fought, 130
Worsted, drove off and did to nothing, perchance.
There may be something quiet o'er His head,
Out of His reach, that feels nor joy nor grief,
Since both derive from weakness in some way.
I joy because the quails come; would not joy

Could I bring quails here when I have a mind:
This Quiet, all it hath a mind to, doth.
'Esteemeth stars the outposts of its couch,
But never spends much thought nor care that way.
It may look up, work up, – the worse for those   140
It works on! 'Careth but for Setebos
The many-handed as a cuttle-fish,
Who, making Himself feared through what He does,
Looks up, first, and perceives he cannot soar
To what is quiet and hath happy life;
Next looks down here, and out of very spite
Makes this a bauble-world to ape yon real,
These good things to match those as hips do grapes.
'Tis solace making baubles, ay, and sport.
Himself peeped late, eyed Prosper at his books   150
Careless and lofty, lord now of the isle:
Vexed, 'stitched a book of broad leaves, arrow-shaped,
Wrote thereon, he knows what, prodigious words;
Has peeled a wand and called it by a name;
Weareth at whiles for an enchanter's robe
The eyed skin of a supple oncelot;

And hath an ounce sleeker than youngling mole,
A four-legged serpent he makes cower and couch,
Now snarl, now hold its breath and mind his eye,
And saith she is Miranda and my wife: 160
'Keeps for his Ariel a tall pouch-bill crane
He bids go wade for fish and straight disgorge;
Also a sea-beast, lumpish, which he snared,
Blinded the eyes of, and brought somewhat tame,
And split its toe-webs, and now pens the drudge
In a hole o' the rock and calls him Caliban;
A bitter heart that bides its time and bites.
'Plays thus at being Prosper in a way,
Taketh his mirth with make-believes: so He.

His dam held that the Quiet made all things   170
Which Setebos vexed only: 'holds not so.
Who made them weak, meant weakness He might vex.
Had He meant other, while His hand was in,
Why not make horny eyes no thorn could prick,

Or plate my scalp with bone against the snow,
Or overscale my flesh 'neath joint and joint,
Like an orc's armour? Ay, – so spoil His sport!
He is the One now: only He doth all.

'Saith, He may like, perchance, what profits Him.
Ay, himself loves what does him good; but why?   180
'Gets good no otherwise. This blinded beast
Loves whoso places flesh-meat on his nose,
But, had he eyes, would want no help, but hate
Or love, just as it liked him: He hath eyes.
Also it pleaseth Setebos to work,
Use all His hands, and exercise much craft,
By no means for the love of what is worked.
'Tasteth, himself, no finer good i' the world
When all goes right, in this safe summer-time,
And he wants little, hungers, aches not much,   190
Than trying what to do with wit and strength.
'Falls to make something: 'piled yon pile of turfs,
And squared and stuck there squares of soft white chalk,
And, with a fish-tooth, scratched a moon on each,
And set up endwise certain spikes of tree,
And crowned the whole with a sloth's skull a-top,
Found dead i' the woods, too hard for one to kill.
No use at all i' the work, for work's sole sake;
'Shall some day knock it down again: so He.

'Saith He is terrible: watch His feats in proof!   200
One hurricane will spoil six good months' hope.
He hath a spite against me, that I know,
Just as He favours Prosper, who knows why?
So it is, all the same, as well I find.
'Wove wattles half the winter, fenced them firm
With stone and stake to stop she-tortoises
Crawling to lay their eggs here: well, one wave,
Feeling the foot of Him upon its neck,
Gaped as a snake does, lolled out its large tongue,
And licked the whole labour flat: so much for spite.   210
'Saw a ball flame down late (yonder it lies)
Where, half an hour before, I slept i' the shade:

Often they scatter sparkles: there is force!
'Dug up a newt He may have envied once
And turned to stone, shut up inside a stone.
Please Him and hinder this? – What Prosper does?
Aha, if He would tell me how! Not He!
There is the sport: discover how or die!
All need not die, for of the things o' the isle
Some flee afar, some dive, some run up trees;   220
Those at His mercy, – why, they please Him most
When . . . when . . . well, never try the same way twice!
Repeat what act has pleased, He may grow wroth.
You must not know His ways, and play Him off,
Sure of the issue. 'Doth the like himself:
'Spareth a squirrel that it nothing fears
But steals the nut from underneath my thumb,
And when I threat, bites stoutly in defence:
'Spareth an urchin that contrariwise,
Curls up into a ball, pretending death   230
For fright at my approach: the two ways please.
But what would move my choler more than this,
That either creature counted on its life
To-morrow and next day and all days to come,
Saying, forsooth, in the inmost of its heart,
'Because he did so yesterday with me,
And otherwise with such another brute,
So must he do henceforth and always.' – Ay?
Would teach the reasoning couple what 'must' means!
'Doth as he likes, or wherefore Lord? So He.   .   240

'Conceiveth all things will continue thus,
And we shall have to live in fear of Him
So long as He lives, keeps His strength: no change,
If He have done His best, make no new world
To please Him more, so leave off watching this, –
If He surprise not even the Quiet's self
Some strange day, – or, suppose, grow into it
As grubs grow butterflies: else, here are we,
And there is He, and nowhere help at all.

'Believeth with the life, the pain shall stop.   250

His dam held different, that after death
He both plagued enemies and feasted friends:
Idly! He doth His worst in this our life,
Giving just respite lest we die through pain,
Saving last pain for worst, – with which, an end.
Meanwhile, the best way to escape His ire
Is, not to seem too happy. 'Sees, himself,
Yonder two flies, with purple films and pink,
Bask on the pompion-bell above: kills both.
'Sees two black painful beetles roll their ball   260
On head and tail as if to save their lives:
Moves them the stick away they strive to clear.

Even so, 'would have Him misconceive, suppose
This Caliban strives hard and ails no less,
And always, above all else, envies Him;
Wherefore he mainly dances on dark nights,
Moans in the sun, gets under holes to laugh,
And never speaks his mind save housed as now:
Outside, 'groans, curses. If He caught me here,
O'erheard this speech, and asked 'What chucklest at?'   270
'Would, to appease Him, cut a finger off,
Or of my three kid yearlings burn the best,
Or let the toothsome apples rot on tree,
Or push my tame beast for the orc to taste:
While myself lit a fire, and made a song
And sung it, '*What I hate, be consecrate*
To celebrate Thee and Thy state, no mate
For Thee; what see for envy in poor me?'
Hoping the while, since evils sometimes mend,
Warts rub away and sores are cured with slime,   280
That some strange day, will either the Quiet catch
And conquer Setebos, or likelier He
Decrepit may doze, doze, as good as die.
[What, what? A curtain o'er the world at once!
Crickets stop hissing; not a bird – or, yes,
There scuds His raven that has told Him all!
It was fool's play, this prattling! Ha! The wind
Shoulders the pillared dust, death's house o' the move,
And fast invading fires begin! White blaze –

A tree's head snaps – and there, there, there, there, there, 290
His thunder follows! Fool to gibe at Him!
Lo! 'Lieth flat and loveth Setebos!
'Maketh his teeth meet through his upper lip,
Will let those quails fly, will not eat this month
One little mess of whelks, so he may 'scape!]

A LIKENESS

Some people hang portraits up
In a room where they dine or sup:
    And the wife clinks tea-things under,
And her cousin, he stirs his cup,
    Asks, 'Who was the lady, I wonder?'
' 'Tis a daub John bought at a sale,'
    Quoth the wife, – looks black as thunder:
'What a shade beneath her nose!
Snuff-taking, I suppose, –'
Adds the cousin, while John's corns ail. 10

Or else, there's no wife in the case,
But the portrait's queen of the place,
    Alone mid the other spoils
Of youth, – masks, gloves and foils,
And pipe-sticks, rose, cherry-tree, jasmine,
    And the long whip, the tandem-lasher,
And the cast from a fist ('not, alas! mine,
    But my master's, the Tipton Slasher'),
And the cards where pistol-balls mark ace,
And a satin shoe used for cigar-case, 20
And the chamois-horns ('shot in the Chablais')
    And prints – Rarey drumming on Cruiser,
    And Sayers, our champion, the bruiser,
And the little edition of Rabelais:
Where a friend, with both hands in his pockets,
    May saunter up close to examine it,
    And remark a good deal of Jane Lamb in it,
'But the eyes are half out of their sockets;
That hair's not so bad, where the gloss is,
But they've made the girl's nose a proboscis: 30

Jane Lamb, that we danced with at Vichy!
What, is not she Jane? Then, who is she?'

All that I own is a print,
An etching, a mezzotint;
'Tis a study, a fancy, a fiction,
Yet a fact (take my conviction)
Because it has more than a hint
   Of a certain face, I never
Saw elsewhere touch or trace of
In women I've seen the face of: 40
   Just an etching, and, so far, clever.

I keep my prints, an imbroglio,
Fifty in one portfolio.
When somebody tries my claret,
We turn round chairs to the fire,
Chirp over days in a garret,
   Chuckle o'er increase of salary,
Taste the good fruits of our leisure,
Talk about pencil and lyre,
   And the National Portrait Gallery: 50
Then I exhibit my treasure.
After we've turned over twenty,
   And the debt of wonder my crony owes
   Is paid to my Marc Antonios,
He stops me – 'Festina lentè!
What's that sweet thing there, the etching?'
How my waistcoat-strings want stretching,
   How my cheeks grow red as tomatoes,
How my heart leaps! But hearts, after leaps, ache.

'By the by, you must take, for a keepsake,   60
   That other, you praised, of Volpato's.'
The fool! would he try a flight further and say –
He never saw, never before to-day,
What was able to take his breath away,
A face to lose youth for, to occupy age
With the dream of, meet death with, – why, I'll not engage
But that, half in a rapture and half in a rage,

I should toss him the thing's self—' 'Tis only a duplicate,
A thing of no value! Take it, I supplicate!'

EPILOGUE

First Speaker, as David

I

On the first of the Feast of Feasts,
   The Dedication Day,
When the Levites joined the Priests
   At the Altar in robed array,
Gave signal to sound and say, —

II

When the thousands, rear and van,
   Swarming with one accord
Became as a single man
   (Look, gesture, thought and word)
In praising and thanking the Lord, —   10

III

When the singers lift up their voice,
   And the trumpets made endeavour,
Sounding, 'In God rejoice!'
   Saying, 'In Him rejoice
Whose mercy endureth for ever!' —

IV

Then the Temple filled with a cloud,
   Even the House of the Lord;
Porch bent and pillar bowed:
   For the presence of the Lord,
In the glory of His cloud,   20
   Had filled the House of the Lord.

140

Second Speaker, as Renan

Gone now! All gone across the dark so far,
   Sharpening fast, shuddering ever, shutting still,
Dwindling into the distance, dies that star
   Which came, stood, opened once! We gazed our fill
With upturned faces on as real a Face
   That, stooping from grave music and mild fire,
Took in our homage, made a visible place
   Through many a depth of glory, gyre on gyre,
For the dim human tribute. Was this true?   30
   Could man indeed avail, mere praise of his,
To help by rapture God's own rapture too,
   Thrill with a heart's red tinge that pure pale bliss?
Why did it end? Who failed to beat the breast,
   And shriek, and throw the arms protesting wide,
When a first shadow showed the star addressed
   Itself to motion, and on either side
The rims contracted as the rays retired;
   The music, like a fountain's sickening pulse,
Subsided on itself; awhile transpired   40
   Some vestige of a Face no pangs convulse,
No prayers retard; then even this was gone,
   Lost in the night at last. We, lone and left
Silent through centuries, ever and anon
   Venture to probe again the vault bereft
Of all now save the lesser lights, a mist
   Of multitudinous points, yet suns, men say –
And this leaps ruby, this lurks amethyst,
   But where may hide what came and loved our clay?
How shall the sage detect in yon expanse   50
   The star which chose to stoop and stay for us?
Unroll the records! Hailed ye such advance
   Indeed, and did your hope evanish thus?
Watchers of twilight, is the worst averred?
   We shall not look up, know ourselves are seen,
Speak, and be sure that we again are heard,
   Acting or suffering, have the disk's serene
Reflect our life, absorb an earthly flame,
   Nor doubt that, were mankind inert and numb,

Its core had never crimsoned all the same,   60
    Nor, missing ours, its music fallen dumb?
Oh, dread succession to a dizzy post,
    Sad sway of sceptre whose mere touch appals,
Ghastly dethronement, cursed by those the most
    On whose repugnant brow the crown next falls!

Third Speaker

I

Witless alike of will and way divine,
How heaven's high with earth's low should intertwine!
Friends, I have seen through your eyes: now use mine!

II

Take the least man of all mankind, as I;
Look at his head and heart, find how and why   70
He differs from his fellows utterly:

III

Then, like me, watch when nature by degrees
Grows alive round him, as in Arctic seas
(They said of old) the instinctive water flees

IV

Toward some elected point of central rock,
As though, for its sake only, roamed the flock
Of waves about the waste: awhile they mock

V

With radiance caught for the occasion, – hues
Of blackest hell now, now such reds and blues
As only heaven could fitly interfuse, –   80

The mimic monarch of the whirlpool, king
O' the current for a minute: then they wring
Up by the roots and oversweep the thing,

And hasten off, to play again elsewhere
The same part, choose another peak as bare,
They find and flatter, feast and finish there.

When you see what I tell you, – nature dance
About each man of us, retire, advance,
As though the pageant's end were to enhance

His worth, and – once the life, his product, gained –   90
Roll away elsewhere, keep the strife sustained,
And show thus real, a thing the North but feigned –

When you acknowledge that one world could do
All the diverse work, old yet ever new,
Divide us, each from other, me from you, –

Why, where's the need of Temple, when the walls
O' the world are that? What use of swells and falls
From Levites' choir, Priests' cries, and trumpet-calls?

That one Face, far from vanish, rather grows,
Or decomposes but to recompose,   100
Become my universe that feels and knows.

Such Poems as the following come properly enough, I suppose, under the head of 'Dramatic Pieces;' being, though for the most part Lyric in expression, always Dramatic in principle, and so many utterances of so many imaginary persons, not mine.

R.B.

from LETTER TO ELIZABETH BARRETT
(13 January 1845)

Dear Miss Barrett,

. . . your poetry must be, cannot but be, infinitely more to me than mine to you – for you *do* what I always wanted, hoped to do, and only seem now likely to do for the first time. You speak out, *you*, – I only make men & women speak – give you truth broken into prismatic hues, and fear the pure white light, even if it is in me: but I am going to try. . . .

Ever yours most faithfully
R. Browning

from LETTER TO ELIZABETH BARRETT
(11 February 1845)

Dear Miss Barrett,

. . . what I have printed gives *no* knowledge of me – it evidences abilities of various kinds, if you will – and a dramatic sympathy with certain modifications of passion . . . *that* I think: but I never have begun, even, what I hope I was born to begin and end, – 'R.B. a poem.' And, next, if I speak (and, God knows, feel) as if what you have read were sadly imperfect demonstrations of even mere ability, it is from no absurd vanity, tho' it might seem so – these scenes and song–scraps *are* such mere and very escapes of my inner power, which lives in me like the light in those crazy Mediterranean phares I have watched at sea – wherein the light is ever revolving in a dark gallery, bright and alive, and

10

only after a weary interval leaps out, for a moment, from the one narrow chink, and then goes on with the blind wall between it and you; and, no doubt, *then*, precisely, does the poor drudge that carries the cresset set himself most busily to trim the wick – for don't think I want to say I have not worked hard – (this head of mine knows better) – but the work has been *inside*, and not when at stated times I held up   20
my light to you – and, that there is no self-delusion here, I would prove to you, (and nobody else) even by opening this desk I write on, and showing what stuff, in the way of wood, I *could* make a great bonfire with, if I might only knock the whole clumsy top off my tower! – Of course, every writing body says the same, so I gain nothing by the avowal; but when I remember how I have done what was published, and half done what may never be, I say with some right, you can know but little of me. . . .

. . . know me for yours ever faithfully,   30

R. Browning

from ESSAY ON SHELLEY (1852)

.   .   .

Doubtless we accept gladly the biography of an objective poet, as the phrase now goes; one whose endeavour has been to reproduce things external (whether the phenomena of the scenic universe, or the manifested action of the human heart and brain) with an immediate reference, in every case, to the common eye and apprehension of his fellow men, assumed capable of receiving and profiting by this reproduction. It has been obtained through the poet's double faculty of seeing external objects more clearly, widely, and deeply, than is possible to the average mind, at the same time that he   10
is so acquainted and in sympathy with its narrower comprehension as to be careful to supply it with no other materials than it can combine into an intelligible whole. The auditory of such a poet will include, not only the intelligences which, save for such assistance, would have missed the deeper meaning and enjoyment of the original objects, but also the spirits of a like endowment with his own, who, by means of

his abstract, can forthwith pass to the reality it was made from, and either corroborate their impressions of things known already, or supply themselves with new from what- 20 ever shows in the inexhaustible variety of existence may have hitherto escaped their knowledge. Such a poet is properly the ποιητης, the fashioner; and the thing fashioned, his poetry, will of necessity be substantive, projected from himself and distinct. . . .

Doubtless, with respect to such a poet, we covet his biography. We desire to look back upon the process of gathering together in a lifetime, the materials of the work we behold entire. . . . Still, fraught with instruction and interest as such details undoubtedly are, we can, if needs be, 30 dispense with them. The man passes, the work remains. The work speaks for itself, as we say. . . .

We turn with stronger needs to the genius of an apposite tendency – the subjective poet of modern classification. He, gifted like the objective poet with the fuller perception of nature and man, is impelled to embody the thing he per- ceives, not so much with reference to the many below as to the One above him, the supreme Intelligence which apprehends all things in their absolute truth, – an ultimate view ever aspired to, if but partially attained, by the poet's 40 own soul. Not what man sees, but what God sees – the *Ideas* of Plato, seeds of creation lying burningly on the Divine Hand – it is toward these that he struggles. Not with the combination of humanity in action, but with the primal elements of humanity he has to do; and he digs where he stands, – preferring to seek them in his own soul as the nearest reflex of that absolute Mind, according to the in- tuitions of which he desires to perceive and speak. Such a poet does not deal habitually with the picturesque group- ings and tempestuous tossings of the forest-trees, but with 50 their roots and fibres naked to the chalk and stone. He does not paint pictures and hang them on the walls, but rather carries them on the retina of his own eyes: we must look deep into his human eyes, to see those pictures on them. He is rather a seer, accordingly, than a fashioner, and what he produces will be less a work than an effluence. That efflu- ence cannot be easily considered in abstraction from his personality, – being indeed the very radiance and aroma of his personality, projected from it but not separated. . . .

I shall observe, in passing, that it seems not so much from any essential distinction in the faculty of the two poets or in the nature of the objects contemplated by either, as in the more immediate adaptability of these objects to the distinct purpose of each, that the objective poet, in his appeal to the aggregate human mind, chooses to deal with the doings of men, (the result of which dealing, in its pure form, when even description, as suggesting a describer, is dispensed with, is what we call dramatic poetry), while the subjective poet, whose study has been himself, appealing through himself to the absolute Divine mind, prefers to dwell upon those external scenic appearances which strike out most abundantly and uninterruptedly his inner light and power, selects that silence of the earth and sea in which he can best hear the beating of his individual heart, and leaves the noisy, complex, yet imperfect exhibitions of nature in the manifold experience of man around him, which serve only to distract and suppress the working of his brain. . . . It would be idle to inquire, of these two kinds of poetic faculty in operation, which is the higher or even rarer endowment. If the subjective might seem to be the ultimate requirement of every age, the objective, in the strictest state, must still retain its original value. For it is with this world, as starting point and basis alike, that we shall always have to concern ourselves: the world is not to be learned and thrown aside, but reverted to and relearned. The spiritual comprehension may be infinitely subtilised, but the raw material it operates upon, must remain. There may be no end of the poets who communicate to us what they see in an object with reference to their own individuality; what it was before they saw it, in reference to the aggregate human mind, will be as desirable to know as ever. Nor is there any reason why these two modes of poetic faculty may not issue hereafter from the same poet in successive perfect works, examples of which, according to what are now considered the exigences of art, we have hitherto possessed in distinct individuals only. A mere running in of the one faculty upon the other, is, of course, the ordinary circumstance. Far more rarely it happens that either is found so decidedly prominent and superior, as to be pronounced comparatively pure: while of the perfect shield, with the gold and the silver side set up for all comers to challenge, there has yet been no instance. Either faculty in its eminent state is doubtless conceded by Providence as a best gift to men, according to their especial want. There is a time when the general eye has, so to speak, absorbed its fill of the phenomena around it, whether spiritual or material, and desires rather to learn the exacter significance of what it possesses, than to receive any augmentation of what is possessed. Then is the opportunity for the poet of loftier vision, to lift his fellows, with their half-apprehensions, up to his own sphere, by intensifying the import of details and rounding the universal meaning. The influence of such an achievement will not soon die out. A tribe of successors (Homerides) working more or less in the same spirit, dwell on his discoveries and reinforce his doctrine; till, at unawares, the world is found to be subsisting wholly on the shadow of a reality, on sentiments diluted from passions, on the tradition of a fact, the convention of a moral, the straw of last year's harvest. Then is the imperative call for the appearance of another sort of poet, who shall at once replace this intellectual rumination of food swallowed long ago, by a supply of the fresh and living swathe; getting at new substance by breaking up the assumed wholes into parts of independent and unclassed value, careless of the unknown laws for recombining them (it will be the business of yet another poet to suggest those hereafter), prodigal of objects for men's outer and not inner sight, shaping for their uses a new and different creation from the last, which it displaces by the right of life over death, – to endure until, in the inevitable process, its very sufficiency to itself shall require, at length, an exposition of its affinity to something higher, – when the positive yet conflicting facts shall again precipitate themselves under a harmonising law, and one more degree will be apparent for a poet to climb in that mighty ladder, of which, however cloud-involved and undefined may glimmer the topmost step, the world dares no longer doubt that its gradations ascend.

. . .

from LETTER TO JOHN RUSKIN
(10 December 1855)

My dear Ruskin,

. . . We don't read poetry the same way, by the same law; it is too clear. I cannot begin writing poetry till my imaginary reader has conceded licences to me which you demur at altogether. I *know* that I don't make out my conception by my language, all poetry being a putting the infinite within the finite. You would have me paint it all plain out, which can't be; but by various artifices I try to make shift with touches and bits of outlines which *succeed* if they bear the conception from me to you. You ought, I think, to keep   10
pace with the thought tripping from ledge to ledge of my 'glaciers,' as you call them; not stand poking your alpen-stock into the holes, and demonstrating that no foot could have stood there; – suppose it sprang over there? In *prose* you may criticize so – because that is the absolute representation of portions of truth, what chronicling is to history – but in asking for more *ultimates* you must accept less *mediates*, nor expect that a Druid stone-circle will be traced for you with as few breaks to the eye as the North Crescent and South Crescent that go together so cleverly in many a suburb. . . .   20
. . . I *may* put Robert Browning into Pippa and other men and maids. If so, *peccavi* ['I have sinned']: but I don't see myself in them, at all events.

Do you think poetry was ever generally understood – or can be? Is the business of it to tell people what they know already, as they know it, and so precisely that they shall be able to cry out – 'Here you should supply *this* – *that*, you evidently pass over, and I'll help you from my own stock'? It is all teaching, on the contrary, and the people hate to be taught. They say otherwise, – make foolish fables about   30
Orpheus enchanting stocks and stones, poets standing up and being worshipped, – all nonsense and impossible dreaming. . . .

Yours ever faithfully,
Robert Browning

PREFACE TO *THE POETICAL WORKS* (1868)

The poems that follow are printed in the order of their publication. The first piece in the series [*Pauline*], I acknowledge and retain with extreme repugnance, indeed purely of necessity; for not long ago I inspected one, and am certified of the existence of other transcripts, intended sooner or later to be published abroad: by forestalling these, I can at least correct some misprints (no syllable is changed) and introduce a boyish work by an exculpatory word. The thing was my earliest attempt at 'poetry always dramatic in principle, and so many utterances of so many imaginary persons, not mine,' which I have since written according to a scheme less extravagant and scale less impracticable than were ventured upon in this crude preliminary sketch – a sketch that, on reviewal, appears not altogether wide of some hint of the characteristic features of that particular *dramatis persona* it would fain have reproduced: good draughtsmanship, however, and right handling were far beyond the artist at that time.

R.B.

London, December 25, 1867.

Critical Commentary

In Wordsworth's 'Ode: Intimations of Immortality From Recollections of Early Childhood' the poet–speaker tells us that in early childhood he had apprehensions of the divine origin of the human soul: 'trailing clouds of glory do we come / From God, who is our home: / Heaven lies about us in our infancy!' (ll.64–6). But, from his perspective in the present, the 'visionary gleam' (l. 56) of childhood has faded. We are told, moreover, how an immediate sense of the infinite *necessarily* recedes as individual personality forms amidst the divisions and multiplicities of earthly life: 'Shades of the prison-house begin to close / Upon the growing Boy . . .' (ll. 67–8). Yet all is not lost, since the poet–speaker insists that those early visions of the 'eternal mind' (l. 113) hold still – through all the mediations of experience – a defining authority over the adult imagination. They provide still an absolute cognitive frame of reference, organizing experience itself. They are

> yet the fountain-light of all our day,
> Are yet a master-light of all our seeing;
> > Uphold us, cherish, and have power to make
> Our noisy years seem moments in the being
> Of the eternal Silence: truths that wake,
> > To perish never . . .

> > > > > (155–60)

By contrast, there is in Browning's work no such confidently affirmative vision of the transactions between the 'One above' and the 'many below' (to use his own expression from his 1852

151

'Essay on Shelley'; Brett-Smith 1921: p. 65). As noted in the Introduction, Browning's poetry turns, in general, on a sense of the difficulty of matching multiplicity with some grand, totalizing scheme of thought and belief about the world; and, in particular, on an unease concerning Romantic idealist psychology and metaphysics. Certainly there is in Browning's verse an examination of the ordering processes of the mind. But the emphasis is not on the availability or achievement of an absolute vision, of an ultimately stable paradigm which incorporates and resolves disparateness and doubt. There is, instead, a repeated witness to something much more provisional and relative. Browning gives such witness in poems that are characteristically densely impacted and complex and which above all else demand very close reading. There is, of course, insufficient space in the following pages to pursue extensively this kind of reading. But something of the close attention to textual detail required by Browning's verse must be paid initially to at least some instances of his poetic preoccupation with the provisional and relative. And a good first example of that preoccupation is the dramatic lyric 'Two in the Campagna' from *Men and Women*.

In 'Two in the Campagna' a speaker addresses a lover as they walk or stray through the Roman countryside in spring. The poem opens with a question:

> I wonder do you feel to-day
>   As I have felt since, hand in hand,
> We sat down on the grass, to stray
>   In spirit better through the land,
> This morn of Rome and May?

Apparently just one occasion is being referred to here ('to-day', 'This morn'). The speaker is asking his lover if she feels as he has been feeling since, in the course of their morning walk, they sat down together on the grass. The reason for sitting down may be that wandering in the mind is better than literally walking, or it may be that pausing awhile for spiritual refreshment makes the actual walk a better one. The syntax is slippery and tentative, but not gratuitously so. For the awkwardness of the syntax is already enacting what will turn out to be the central preoccupation of the poem: the difficulty, that is, of establishing a clear and permanent order in the life of the mind.

Not that 'Two in the Campagna' is concerned to suggest that the mind is simply a chaos. In the succeeding three stanzas, as the speaker describes his own thoughts on 'This morn', the poem imagines the way in which even extremely elusive thoughts and associations may be discriminated and apprehended. The movements of the mind are understood in these lines by analogy with the complex ramifications of a gossamer web. Yet it is a web that is not entirely untraceable, as the speaker pursues and finally holds a particular thought as one might pursue a skein of spider's web to its conclusion:

> For me, I touched a thought, I know,
> 　　Has tantalized me many times,
> (Like turns of thread the spiders throw
> 　　Mocking across our path) for rhymes
> To catch at and let go.
>
> Help me to hold it! First it left
> 　　The yellowing fennel, run to seed
> There, branching from the brickwork's cleft,
> 　　Some old tomb's ruin: yonder weed
> Took up the floating weft,
>
> Where one small orange cup amassed
> 　　Five beetles, – blind and green they grope
> Among the honey-meal: and last,
> 　　Everywhere on the grassy slope
> I traced it. Hold it fast!

This sequence affirms the possibility of recognizing some kind of continuity and of establishing some kind of stable position in the life of the mind. But the verse equally contains much that suggests the precariousness of such continuity and stability. There is, in the first place, the leading figure of gossamer, with its connotations of refined strength, yet also of delicate vulnerability and even of potential, subtle entrapment. Then there is the reference to the attempt at fixing the elusive 'thought' in rhyme – where the achievement of poetic form is understood as a type of the ordering powers of the mind. But not only is poetic expression of the thought difficult ('tantalized me . . . for rhymes'), the order that is gained through poetic articulation is itself seen as something which must be relinquished almost as soon as it is achieved ('To catch at and let go').

This sense of precariousness is something that is deepened in the fundamental contrast that is set up throughout the passage between the control exemplified in the tracing of a thought and the randomness, even the rampancy, of natural life. Just as a thought is pictured in terms of a gossamer thread, so the vegetative and animal life across which the thread of thought runs also bears a figurative significance in respect of the life of the mind. Put in specifically psychological terms, the relationship between the act of tracing a thread of thought and the natural life through which the thought is pursued is one that dramatizes the relationship between conscious and controlled dimensions of the psyche, on the one hand, and uncontrolled or, perhaps, unconscious dimensions, on the other. As far as the latter are concerned, some of the connotations in this passage – those arising from the richness and variety of natural forms – are positive. But there are at once more disturbing psychological possibilities figured in the random play of natural energy: connotations, that is, of simultaneous exhaustion and promiscuous fertility ('run to seed'); or of ignorant and directionless will ('blind and green they grope'). The arbitrary principle by which conscious mental connections and transitions are sustained also implicitly threatens the continuities that are affirmed. The imagery suggests that the development of a thought may be achieved by a force that is itself uncultivated, one that lies outside the directed and the predictable ('yonder weed/ Took up the floating weft'). Overall, the details of the second to fourth stanzas add up to a composite image of the psyche as not simply in unity with itself, its drive towards control existing in uncertain relation with unmanaged and unmanageable forces. It is not an uncertainty that is ever completely resolved. Yet beneath the insistence on the process of ordering there is, in the picture of a failed piece of human architecture, an implication that the mind's attempt at structuring may, in the last resort, be invaded and overwhelmed by those uncontained psychic drives that are associated with untrammelled natural growth ('branching from the brickwork's cleft / Some old tomb's ruin').

Such an implication becomes the explicit preoccupation of the remainder of 'Two in the Campagna'. From the moment of controlling the 'thought' at the end of stanza four the speaker opens out into a consideration of the nature of human love. This consideration is itself apparently the difficult and elusive 'thought' which the speaker has succeeded in tracking down. Certainly it reproduces – although within a different scope of reference and with a different emphasis – the terms that have been introduced in stanzas two to four. We find the speaker observing in stanza six, for example, the spontaneous fullness of the natural life of the campagna:

> Such life here, through such lengths of hours,
>   Such miracles performed in play,
> Such primal naked forms of flowers,
>   Such letting nature have her way . . .

This kind of observation modulates in the seventh stanza into a reflection on the dynamics of human love. The speaker makes the point that in contrast with the unconfined generative impulses of nature ('primal naked forms'), human sexual love is somehow subject to a regulatory and limiting mechanism. Having eulogized nature's blissful lack of self-control the speaker frustratedly queries the presence in human nature of a self-regulating power: 'How is it under our control / To love or not to love?' Why is it that, in contrast with pure spontaneity, human nature apparently inherits a capacity to apportion love? Stanza eight restates the speaker's wish that human love might be as uncircumscribed as the life of nature, while at the same time acknowledging that such circumscription, however damaging, is nevertheless a necessary condition of human nature. So necessary that, although its cause or origin are inexplicable, it is described in terms ('fault' and 'wound') which parallel Christian terms of describing the fallen state of human nature.[1] In these lines the human power of control and restriction is like some penalty of the Fall, the factor which excludes human beings from participation in the unselfconscious, paradisal freedom of natural life:

> I would that you were all to me,
>   You that are just so much, no more.
> Nor yours nor mine, nor slave nor free!
>   Where does the fault lie? What the core
> O' the wound, since wound must be?

The problem can again be described in the light of a psychological model that sees a split between uncontrolled and controlled sides of the psyche. If human beings could be unself-consciously instinctive in the manner of natural life then all might be well. But the self-conscious ego upon which the nature of being a human individual depends is something that exists by setting boundaries and limits. Indeed it doesn't simply *set* these. Control is not merely a capacity of the conscious self, it is part of the very constitution of that self. For that self is born of separation and of the controls inherent in that state. It is defined by difference and hence by relativity and finitude. And what stops total fulfilment in human love is the requirement of the individual ego that it remain itself, bound by the limits that constitute it. Ultimately unconditioned union with another – the fantasy of romantic love – thus becomes an impossibility within mortal life. The conscious self cannot transcend its own delimited and finite nature without contradicting its very being. For the conscious self finally to abandon the limits and control that define it would be to cancel itself, so that while it may yearn for or fantasize absolute oneness with another it automatically draws a line against it. The further 'wound' here, of course, is that control in this sense does not manifest itself as a matter of choice. Such control is never simply under control: it lies beyond the power of regulation as a capacity of the conscious self. And this is the additional import of the speaker's question, 'How is it under our control . . . ?':

> I would that you were all to me,
>   You that are just so much, no more . . .
>
> I would I could adopt your will,
>   See with your eyes, and set my heart
> Beating by yours, and drink my fill
>   At your soul's springs, – your part my part
> In life, for good or ill.

But 'No . . .', reflects the speaker in the following stanza as he begins to define the sense in which such interchangeableness is unavailable for the human lover. Except in the context of some suicidal love-pact, the individual lover will by definition never be in the position utterly to let him or herself go. Stanzas ten to eleven emphasize how, in the normal field of human love, communion and fulfilment are always limited, transitory:

No. I yearn upward, touch you close,
    Then stand away. I kiss your cheek,
Catch your soul's warmth, – I pluck the rose
    And love it more than tongue can speak –
Then the good minute goes.

Already how am I so far
    Out of that minute? Must I go
Still like the thistle-ball, no bar,
    Onward, whenever light winds blow,
Fixed by no friendly star?

This sense of an unavoidable loss of completeness in love stands in the poem as a type of the general human drive towards fulfilment: the human condition is envisaged as one in which fixed and absolute positions are endlessly sought even as they endlessly recede. But what has happened in these latter verses is a reversal of the insistence on the ordering powers of the mind which was apparent in stanzas two to four ('Help me to hold it'). As the speaker traces through his thought about the disjunction between nature's freedom and the regulation inherent in human love there is a discovery that it is the control of thought which enforces the disjunction. The thing that was so desperately sought in the earlier stanzas turns out to be the thing that is most resented in the later ones. The realization is that the human drive to control, bound by finitude, brings no total resolution, for it banishes absolute fullness precisely by drawing lines and establishing limits.

It is, then, a painfully apprehended paradox in 'Two in the Campagna' that human formulations of order and stability yield, in their partiality, only further disorder and instability. And as the ordering drive is inalienably a part of being human the mind has to be envisaged as committed to exercises in control that can only ever be provisional and relative. The point applies, of course, even to the poem itself as an expression of the desire to establish pattern. The controlled exploration of a difficult thought that forms the subject of this poem does not itself bring any con-summatory insight or resolution. In the final stanza the poem circles back on itself as it admits that its own formulation of control is but a stage in a ceaseless process of formulation and reformulation of order. We are a long way from Wordsworth's 'truths that wake, / To perish never' as 'Two in the Campagna' concludes without asserting the possibility of closure. It is a lack of closure that defines the endless cycle of desire upon which human life is predicated:

> Just when I seemed about to learn!
>   Where is the thread now? Off again!
> The old trick! Only I discern —
>   Infinite passion, and the pain
> Of finite hearts that yearn.

'Off again!' It is a note struck time and again, in a wide range of contexts with a wide range of emphases, in Browning's poetry. Thus James Lee's wife, in the poem of that name from *Dramatis Personae*, is found slowly coming to terms with the passing of the completeness she once felt she shared with her husband ('The man was my whole world', l. 109). As she recognizes the partiality and transitoriness of mortal fulfilment and casts around for a new thread to follow, she negotiates different possible responses to a world that is devoid of absolutely fixed points:

> . . . when the wind begins among the vines,
>   So low, so low, what shall it say but this?
> 'Here is the change beginning, here the lines
>   Circumscribe beauty, set to bliss
> The limit time assigns.' . . .

> . . . Why this is the old woe o' the world;
>   Tune, to whose rise and fall we live and die.
> Rise with it, then! Rejoice that man is hurled
>   From change to change unceasingly,
> His soul's wings never furled!

> That's a new question; still replies the fact,
>   Nothing endures: the wind moans, saying so;
> We moan in acquiescence . . .

> (207–11, 217–24)

Browning's poems themselves may sometimes mourn – but they never moan – the pain of human yearning for an end that will not come this side of death. Often, indeed, as in works such as 'Love in a Life' and 'Life in a Love' from *Men and Women*, they are committed to rising with it, to celebrating, even while noting the reality of suffering, the lack of closure in mortal life. In this pair of pendant poems a lovers' relationship becomes a figure specifically of the nature of individual personality. In the first of the two, 'Love in a Life', the speaker is represented, in the words of Mrs Orr, 'as inhabiting the same house with his unseen love; and pursuing her in it ceaselessly from room to room, always catching the flutter of her retreating presence, always sure that the next moment he will overtake her' (Orr 1896: p. 228). The 'unseen love' of this poem, never literally present or available, takes on symbolic properties as the object of a spiritual or psychological search. It is in this sense that Paul Turner speaks of the poem as an allegory of 'the pursuit of the unattainable' (Turner 1972: p. 332). As such, it is a pursuit that may be wearing but which, as the closing lines of the last stanza reveal, is also submitted to with feelings of pleasure and excitement:

> Yet the day wears . . .
> Still the same chance! she goes out as I enter.
> Spend my whole day in the quest, – who cares?
> But 'tis twilight, you see, – with such suites to explore,
> Such closets to search, such alcoves to importune!
>
> (9, 13–16)

The second poem, 'Life in a Love', emphasizes even more than the first the psychologically self-referential dimension of the allegory. The relationship between the speaker and loved-one here becomes a relation between self and Other, where the 'unseen lover' is a kind of second self of the speaker himself. She is almost the masculine speaker's *anima*, though her status as an anima-figure is not realized as concretely as, say, the 'veiled maid' of Shelley's 'Alastor', whose voice is heard as the 'voice' of the 'soul' of the poet who pursues her (ll. 151, 153); or as Shelley's Emily in 'Epipsychidion' who is spoken of by the speaker as 'soul out of my soul' (l. 238). At any rate, as the object of the speaker's quest, the 'unseen love' of 'Life in a Love' becomes a crucial term in a process of self-definition. Just as human formulations of control and order are seen as provisional in 'Two in the Campagna', so here the self is seen not as a stable, completed entity but as something caught up in an unceasing process of definition. It is envisaged as something unfinished, bound to an activity of making and re-making itself. The speaker of 'Life in a Love' aims to close with his loved-one. Such a closure would be a completion or fulfilment of the self. But it would also be in a literal sense a finishing or an end of the self. For the achievement of a completely resolved self would be to surpass the finite and relative boundaries within which individual human personality – individuated and hence by definition incomplete – takes shape and has its being. Thus it is that the self in 'Life in a Love' is presented as a subject that is inseparable from process, that is constituted in the very search for stability and completion and for whom the attainment of those ends would be tantamount to a removal from life. It is in this conceptual and imaginative context that the speaker of the poem defines the purpose of life not as the reaching of an end but as the activity of moving towards an end. And while the poem recognizes the difficulty of living within such conditions of identity, it more powerfully registers an exhilarated sense of the resilience with which such conditions may be embraced. The inversion in this poem's title, from the 'Love in a Life' of the first poem to 'Life in a Love', endorses this sense of celebration. By this inversion, the compulsive dynamic of life as process, as a matter of generation and regeneration, is identified as the principle of love itself:

> Escape me?
> Never –
> Beloved!
> While I am I, and you are you . . .
> While the one eludes, must the other pursue . . .
> . . . what if I fail of my purpose here?
> It is but to keep the nerves at strain,
>   To dry one's eyes and laugh at a fall,
> And, baffled, get up and begin again, –
>   So the chace takes up one's life, that's all . . .
> No sooner the old hope goes to ground
>   Than a new one, straight to the self-same mark,

I shape me –
Ever
Removed!

(1–4, 7, 11–15, 18–22)

'I shape me'. The aesthetic resonance of this phrase touches something frequently developed by Browning in poems whose speakers are actually artists in one medium or another. The dramatic monologue 'Fra Lippo Lippi' (*Men and Women*), for example, takes as its speaker the Florentine Renaissance painter–monk of that name. The dramatic situation of the poem has Lippo giving an account of himself to members of the Florentine city-guard who have apprehended him as he returns home after a night's revelry. 'I am poor brother Lippo' exclaims the painter in the opening line of the poem. But he follows this up in l. 14 with a further, rhetorical, retort to the guard's implied questioning: 'Who am I?' Returning the guard's question in the form of a question sets the terms of a monologue which turns on the problem that there is no easy definition of what the self is. Lippo's speech becomes an exercise in self-exposition as he summarizes his life's history, telling what he sees himself as having been in the past and as being in the present. But the monologue amounts to a stream – practically a flood – of consciousness in which Lippo never really arrives at a final, stable point in his attempts to define himself. What Lippo might ultimately *be* slips the measure of either himself or of those who would seek to stamp and label him ('you think you see a monk!', l. 3; 'Yes, I'm the painter, since you style me so', l. 39). The process is brought to a head, though not to a conclusion, towards the end of the poem as Lippo imagines a standard religious picture that he has been commissioned to produce:

I shall paint
God in the midst, Madonna and her babe,
Ringed by a bowery flowery angel-brood . . .

(347–9)

No sooner, however, has Lippo projected this conventionally patterned and precious ('bowery flowery') picture than he begins, in imagination, to overload it with detail ('then i' the front, of course a saint or two . . .', l. 353; 'And Job, I must have him there

161

past mistake . . .', l. 357). The breathless crowding in of detail begins to threaten to overwhelm the ordered composition with which he had started. It is a tendency that reaches extraordinary proportions when Lippo at last imagines *himself* as suddenly intruding upon his imagined sacred scene:

> up shall come
> Out of a corner when you least expect . . .
> who but Lippo! I!
> Mazed, motionless and moonstruck – I'm the man! . . .
> I, caught up with my monk's-things by mistake . . .
> I, in this presence, this pure company!
> Where's a hole, where's a corner for escape?
>
> (360–1, 363–4, 366, 368–9)

The embarrassing situation is saved by an act of imagination as surprising as that which brought about the situation in the first place. Lippo imagines his disruption and desecration of religious order as being excused by 'a sweet angelic slip of a thing' who defends him against the disapproval of the 'celestial presence' he has himself painted: 'He made you and devised you, after all' (ll. 370, 372–3). So Lippo escapes his own imagined painting, leaving it as a satisfactory, unviolated religious object for the nunnery that commissioned it:

> Thus I scuttle off . . .
> And so all's saved for me, and for the church
> A pretty picture gained.
>
> (383, 388–9)

What is at stake in this entire, humorously absurd flight of fancy is not simply the imagined completion of a painting. Lippo's peculiar incorporation of himself into his painting dramatizes the sense in which a work of art becomes, here as throughout the poem, a figure of the creative and compositional processes of the mind in general. Lippo's being and the activity of painting continually imply each other. The mind and its capacities for making sense of itself and its experience are understood in this poem by analogy with the processes of artistic composition. The point is hinted at early in the poem when Lippo, describing himself as a boy, equates the representational activity of painting not only with other art forms but with the constitutive power of language itself:

> I drew men's faces on my copy-books,
> Scrawled them within the antiphonary's marge,
> Joined legs and arms to the long music-notes,
> Found eyes and nose and chin for A's and B's,
> And made a string of pictures of the world
> Betwixt the ins and outs of verb and noun . . .
>
> (129–34)

Lippo's aesthetic enterprises are not distinguishable from his attempts to make formulations about himself and his experience. Yet he is involved in a process where his endeavour to find a stable structure concerning the self is always failing. Thus, at the end of the poem, he imagines the resolution and stability of a completed painting, but that state of stability and completeness is something that does not contain or define his being. As we witness Lippo imagining the painting it is as if the projective powers of his mind are too great for him to manage them. So abundant is the imagination in this scene that it threatens to undermine the pattern that it does itself create. There is a tension between the mind's capacity to project order and an anarchic principle in the mind which will not be contained by that order. At the last the 'pretty picture' is achieved, 'saved' from disorder, only by the exclusion of the one who brought it into being. Lippo remains outside the order he has created. The concluding line of the poem refers at one level, within the literal dramatic situation of the poem, to the dawn of a new day. But at another level it parallels the 'Off again!' of 'Two in the Campagna' as it carries suggestions of Lippo's need to begin generating another pattern, which will in turn fail to contain the flux of energy that is his imagination and personality: 'There's the grey beginning . . .'.

This whole matter of the formulation and reformulation of structures concerning the self, conceived on an aesthetic model, involves throughout 'Fra Lippo Lippi' a consideration of the relationship between the traditional categories of the sacred and the profane, the religious and the worldly. Lippo is a monk and at once made of 'flesh and blood' (l. 60) and subject to the impulses of the flesh. What Browning does in his portrayal of Lippo is to align his painter's profane impulses with those uncontrolled imaginative energies that repeatedly threaten to subvert the pure orders that the mind would at once produce and take refuge in. So that the contrast between the profane and the sacred is not viewed in this poem in the primarily moral terms of conventional Christian thought. The contrast between the religious and the worldly tends, rather, to be reinterpreted as the contrast between a view that it is possible to achieve a fixed definition of a human being and a recognition of the illusoriness of any such definition. The poem directly mocks the attempt of religion to fit human nature to a permanent mould. The monks who lecture Lippo on the pre-eminence of an anti-naturalist mode in painting trip themselves up as they discover they cannot themselves find a single definition of the nature of the human soul. Much as Lippo slips the order he has imagined in his painting for the nunnery, so the 'soul' escapes the monks' comic attempts to fix it:

> Your business is not to catch men with show,
> With homage to the perishable clay . . .
> Your business is to paint the souls of men –
> Man's soul, and it's a fire, smoke . . . no, it's not . . .
> It's vapour done up like a new-born babe –
> (In that shape when you die it leaves your mouth)
> It's . . . well, what matters talking, it's the soul!
>
> (179–80, 183–7)

Lippo nevertheless still does his painting – striving towards a fixture, even one that he cannot hold himself within. Again, as in 'Life in a Love', Lippo's identity is not identified with any one formulation but is an effect of the effort at formulation. The self here is salvaged or 'saved' through the very act of formulation, but no one self is ever finally formulated or saved. This sense of the self as process rather than as end of course relativizes the religious view of what the self is. It deprives religious definition of an absolute, transcendent status. Throughout 'Fra Lippo Lippi' the possibility opens that religious notions of God are no more than human projections which are questionably claimed as having a more than human authority. It is a possibility that shadows Lippo's account of how he sees the story of the Garden of Eden: 'I always see the garden and God there / A-making man's wife' (ll. 266–7). In the rhetoric of this line God the Creator moves towards being conceived as an artist in the same sense as Lippo is an artist. It is significant in this respect that God as creator (rather than Creator) is not seen simply as having made Eve once and for all time but as 'A-making' her, where the participle suggests not an end but a process. There is a comparable implication in Lippo's statement that he is in a position to interpret God to humanity ('How much more, / If I . . . / Interpret God to all of you!', ll. 308–9, 311), where the idea of being able to interpret God raises the question of whether God can be said to exist independently of interpretation; independently, that is, of human readings or projections.

Such a question is the principal focus of attention in those of Browning's poems which take not artists as speakers but individuals who are directly exploring religious issues. When in the later nineteenth century Browning was admitted to the pantheon of 'major' poets, he entered – as was mentioned in the Introduction – in the face of resistance to the obscurity of his verse and according to the terms of a Victorian cult of the spiritual genius and teacher. For Browning's apologists within this cult the issue of the difficulty of his poetic mode was sidestepped as the verse was translated into prose summaries of its vaunted spiritual and ethical content. In her *Handbook to the Works of Robert Browning* Mrs Orr declared that 'So much of Mr. Browning's moral influence lies in the hopeful religious spirit which his works reveal' (Orr 1896: p. 7). The notion of Browning as a prophet speaking confidently, if not always logically, from a position of spiritual optimism reached a high point in Sir Henry Jones' *Browning as a Philosophical and Religious Teacher* (1891). But it is a notion which survives as a significant dimension of twentieth-century Browning criticism, despite the emergence of critical perspectives which find something more complex in the poetic textures of his work without at the same time disparaging those textures for their difficulty or obscurity.

The idea of Browning as a religious teacher takes, at its most basic level, the spiritual certainty of the speaker of a work such as 'Rabbi Ben Ezra' from *Dramatis Personae* – 'Earth changes, but thy soul and God stand sure' (l. 159) – as no more than the thinly masked utterance of the poet himself. 'Rabbi Ben Ezra', observes one commentator, 'is so much the mouthpiece of Browning himself that it may be asked why the poet thought it necessary to provide an alias' (Pinion 1969: p. 184). Why indeed? But the answer is that this is *not* simply an alias. To ask such a question is gratuitously to forget that 'Rabbi Ben Ezra' is a dramatic monologue, a poem, that is, 'in the first person spoken by, or almost entirely by, someone who is indicated not to be the poet' (Sinfield 1977: p. 8). There is no internal evidence to suggest authorial endorsement of Ben Ezra's voice. No such evidence to imply that the voice of this poem is privileged over the voice of some other monologue in which very different things are said – the voice, say, of 'Cleon' (*Men and Women*). Where Ben Ezra had believed in the objective truth of a God that stands sure, Cleon is sure that revelation of absolute truth may be understood merely as a human creation or fiction:

> Long since, I imaged, wrote the fiction out,
> That he or other god descended here
> And, once for all, showed simultaneously
> What, in its nature, never can be shown,
> Piecemeal or in succession; – showed, I say,
> The worth both absolute and relative
> Of all his children from the birth of time . . .

(115–21)

Now it may be that Cleon's discourse allows us to perceive some of the aridities and limitations of philosophic scepticism. There is no poetic evidence to suggest that Cleon is to be taken as absolutely (and authorially) authoritative. But by the very same token neither is the voice of Ben Ezra. If Ezra has Browning's endorsement, it could be argued with just as much force that so does Cleon when he declares that Christian faith is insane (ll. 350–3). Cleon is frustrated by his own scepticism, just as Karshish (in 'An Epistle . . . of Karshish' from *Men and Women*) is, on the one hand, rationally sceptical about Lazarus' claim to have been raised from the dead but, on the other, expresses a yearning for the emotional fulfilment offered by ideas of a God of Love. Scepticism and emotional or spiritual need are played off against each other within both 'Cleon' and 'Karshish'. But the poems invest imaginative conviction in both sides of the debate they dramatize and neither scepticism nor its opposite are specially privileged within each work, any more than they are in Browning's dramatization of the thought of St John in another 'religious' monologue, 'A Death in the Desert' (*Dramatis*

Personae). Tension and irresolution are the matter of these poems and to suppose that either demonstrates an authorial commitment to the truth or otherwise of the Christian vision is merely to impose a predilection on the poem from outside.

Again, in 'Caliban upon Setebos; or, Natural Theology in the Island' (*Dramatis Personae*), as Caliban constructs an image of God from his experience of himself and of the natural world around him, it is possible to see a satirical attack by Browning on certain contemporary attitudes towards religion – the idea of nineteenth-century Higher Criticism that God is created in the image of man; or, as is suggested in the title of the poem, the idea of the adequacy of a theology based on natural evidence (as against revelation).[2] Once more, however, there is no internal evidence to suggest that such satire is being conducted on the basis of a positive commitment to revealed religion. To read such a commitment in the poem is to construct it according to one set of externally derived terms. Caliban's natural theology may not be meant ironically; or, if ironic, then actually at the expense of those conditioned to think of such theological procedure as somehow erroneous. Rather than a satire, the poem might be taken as a cogent extension of possibilities within Higher Criticism. It could be argued that 'Caliban Upon Setebos' is a portrayal of the fundamental constitution of the human mind and of the way in which *all* human conceptions of experience and of God are produced. The presentation of Caliban as a kind of 'primitive', speaking primarily in the third person, unable to place himself confidently as an 'I', can be taken as an experimental model of a human mind which has not been situated in any particular structure of thought or ideology. What is found through this fantasy model of an unconditioned mind is a given constructive or generative activity, a primordially aesthetic predisposition. And the image Caliban comes up with, of a universe ultimately grounded in indifference and of a world hopelessly perverted and wracked by energies of envy and power, is itself, however rudely formulated, only false if one happens to disagree with it. Within a certain frame of reference, Caliban's tragic vision of the world in relation to the 'Quiet' and 'Setebos' may seem unblinkered and, in principle, deeply sophisticated. Within another frame of reference, all amelioration of such a vision – into notions of a benign divine ordinance – are simply decadent cultural illusions, consolatory fictions of the 'civilized' mind. Patricia Ball has said of Browning's work:

> Wherever God enters the poems, he comes as a property of the speaker's self-made universe: he is not the poet's ulti-mate. . . . this is Browning's point about the human con-dition; and all his people, from Abt Vogler to Mr. Sludge, illustrate it. Each constructs his Setebos, or his Quiet. . . . each awaits confirmation of his own god, his own universe; and no one in the monologues achieves more – or less – in this respect than Caliban on his island.
>
> (Ball 1965: pp. 248–9)

The underlying tendency of Browning's 'religious' poems is towards a suspension of the distinction between art and religion. The difference between Fra Lippo and the various speakers of the religious monologues is not one of kind. Yet the idea of human projection or construction of God is not equatable with a classi-cally reductive scepticism. The 'religious' monologues – by virtue of their dramatic status – are allowed to close neither with strict scepticism nor with traditional religious affirmation. What is opened up implicitly across these monologues and more explicitly in a work such as the 'Epilogue' to *Dramatis Personae* is a space in which the oppositional terms of religious belief and rational scepticism are transgressed. The opening up of this space is inextricably linked with a refusal of the religious dualism of matter and spirit, of world and God. That dualism tends, as the distinction between artistic creation and religious vision dis-solves, to be displaced by a monism in which the divine and the worldly collapse into each other. This is a tendency apparent throughout Browning's work. It traces, for example, everything that Fra Lippo implies – as he resists the view that the representa-tion of soul should be a different thing from that of the body – about the co-inherence of spiritual and material reality. It is also the direct concern of the 'Epilogue' to *Dramatis Personae*, a work which rehearses and reviews the poems of the volume it con-cludes. Of the three speakers in the 'Epilogue', the first, as 'David', articulates the position of a traditional religious faith and observance; the second, as 'Renan', speaks for the sceptical tem-per of the nineteenth century. Both these positions are refused by the third speaker (about as near to an authorial voice as Browning's poetic voices ever come) who asserts that traditional forms of religious belief and modes of sceptical unbelief equally mistake the character of the divine. They mistake it because they both, albeit from different sides of an opposition, maintain a dualistic economy of the spiritual and the material:

> Witless alike of will and way divine,
> How heaven's high with earth's low should intertwine!
>
> (66–7)

A traditional conception of God and a standard scepticism about God, ranging themselves across a divide between spiritual and material worlds, are alike mistaken –

> When you acknowledge that *one* world could do
> All the diverse work, old yet ever new . . .
>
> (93–4; my italics)

What happens in this third speaker's perspective is that religious issue is assimilated to that principle of human imaginative generation and regeneration of pattern which, as we have seen, is emphasized throughout Browning's work. The divine Other (here the 'Face') loses absolute, external, objective reference as it is implicated in the creative processes of mind in experience:

> . . . where's the need of Temple, when the walls
> O' the world are that? . . .
>
> That one Face, far from vanish, rather grows,
> Or decomposes but to recompose,
> Become my universe that feels and knows.
>
> (96–7, 99–101)

While the speaker of these lines celebrates the idea of a dynamic process in which dualistic categories and fixities have no place, the formulation of a monistic and relativistic model moves the celebration beyond the conventional terms of religious affirmation or disaffirmation.

The sacramentalization of the human imagination in a poem such as the 'Epilogue' to *Dramatis Personae* finds an ancestry, of course, in that Romantic internalization of the divine impulse which was summarized earlier in the Introduction. But, as has also been discussed, there is in Browning's work nothing like a high Romantic confidence in the ultimately unconditioned authority and health of the imagination. Creative process in Browning's poetry is explored within a context which does not assume the absolute, transcendent ground of high Romantic belief. The celebratory vitality of a Fra Lippo or even of the third speaker of the 'Epilogue' to *Dramatis Personae* stands relative to the more problematic and pained apprehension of process articulated by the speakers of 'Two in the Campagna' or of 'James Lee's Wife'. Browning's poetry avoids the contradictions inherent in Romantic attempts to link creative activity in the relative and finite realm with a transcendent principle. But in that avoidance it enters an area of dreadful as well as of thrilling possibility. In order to see more clearly how this may be so, it will be useful to turn briefly to Arthur O. Lovejoy's discussion of Western ideas of God in his classic 1936 study, *The Great Chain of Being*.

Lovejoy points out that 'throughout the greater part of its history Western religion, in its more philosophic forms',

> has had two Gods. . . . The two were, indeed, identified as one being with two aspects. But the ideas corresponding to the 'aspects' were ideas of two antithetic kinds of being. The one was the Absolute of otherworldliness – self-sufficient, out of time . . . needing no world of lesser beings to supplement or enhance his own eternal self-contained perfection. The other was a God who emphatically was not self-sufficient nor, in any philosophical sense, 'absolute': one whose essential nature required the existence of other beings . . . a God whose prime attribute was generativeness, whose manifestation was to be found in the diversity of creatures and therefore in the temporal order and the manifold spectacle of nature's processes.
>
> (Lovejoy 1936: p. 315)

God, Lovejoy suggests, cannot be eternally complete and immutable and at once complicit in a universe of contingency and relativity, a universe of generation and process. During the Romantic period, he observes, there emerged a special emphasis on the second idea of God, the idea of God as involved in nature:

> God himself was temporalized – was, indeed, identified with the process by which the whole creation slowly and painfully

ascends the scale of possibility; or, if the name is to be reserved for the summit of the scale, God was conceived as the not yet realized final term of the process. . . . the typically Romantic evolutionism.

(Lovejoy 1936: p. 317)

The ancient contradiction between the two ideas of God continued in much Romantic thinking to be masked as it had always been masked. Frequently in his verse Wordsworth, for example, claims at once an absolute and a relative worth for the imagination. But the pressure of Romantic evolutionism was such as to bring very close a collapse of the long struggle to hold together the two incongruous ideas of the divine. 'The two theologies still subsist side by side; but one of them is a survival, the other is . . . on the point of destroying the former' (Lovejoy 1936: p. 320). It is into a latter world, a world in which that destruction is under way, a world whose parameters are uncertain of absolute guarantees, that Browning's poetry inserts itself.

Even in his critical voice, by no means simply to be confused with his poetic voices, Browning may be found registering a shift of ground away from the absolute idealism of high Romanticism. In his 'Essay on Shelley', he spoke of what he termed the 'subjective' poet as 'impelled to embody the thing he perceives, not so much with reference to the many below as to the One above him, the supreme Intelligence which apprehends all things in their absolute truth' (Brett–Smith 1921: p. 65). Shelley may have been something of this kind of poet, but Browning's sense of his own position is implied when, speaking of the 'objective' poet who engages with the 'many' and who specializes in 'dramatic poetry', he writes of the 'imperative call for the appearance of another sort of poet . . . [who gets at] new substance by breaking up the assumed wholes into parts of independent and unclassed value, careless of the unknown laws for recombining them' (Brett–Smith 1921; pp. 66, 68). In the 'Essay on Shelley' Browning goes on to express a hope that a phase will come when the parts can be recombined and subsumed under a transcendent spiritual whole. In a comparable vein, in a letter of 1845, Browning was happy to imply the reality of an objective truth which Elizabeth Barrett might be able to reach in her verse even if he could not in his own: 'You speak out, *you*, – I only make men &

171

women speak – give you truth broken into prismatic hues, and fear the pure white light, even if it is in me' (Karlin 1989: p. 5). In his critical pronouncements Browning was always to preserve a residue of Romantic aesthetic rhetoric. Thus he wrote in 1855 to Ruskin that 'all poetry' is 'a putting the infinite within the finite' (Cook and Wedderburn 1903–12: XXXVI. p. xxxiv). But he said this in the context of declaring his own inability to do so. And Browning's poetry itself, tirelessly negotiating the 'many', continually discovers the contradictions inherent in attempting to synthesize the many with the 'One'. It is the breaking up of assumed wholes, the destruction of an absolute point of reference for the principle of creativity, that commits Browning's poetry to the expression of simultaneous excitement and profound disturbance. For as Lovejoy also indicates, the temporalizing of God, the destruction of a fixed, objective realm beyond the world of change and process, carried with it a threat to the conception of a comprehensible order to the universe. If the divine that inheres in the world is itself by definition incomplete, implied in a dynamic of becoming that has not yet realized its final term, not yet fulfilled plenitude, then it cannot be taken as a measure of ultimate truth. The rescinding of God's external, absolute status means that

> The realm of possibles is infinite; and the principle of plenitude . . . when *its* implications were thought through, ran on, in every province in which it was applied, into infinities – infinite space, infinite time, infinite worlds, an infinity of existent species, an infinity of individual existences, an infinity of kinds of beings between any two kinds of beings, however similar. When its consequences were thus fully drawn, it confronted the reason of man with a world by which it was not merely baffled but negated; for it was a world of impossible contradictions.
>
> (Lovejoy 1936: p. 331)

It may be possible, on the one hand, to be joyfully careless of the unknown laws for recombining into a whole the many parts of the universe but, on the other, it is also possible to be terrified at the prospect of a realm of unbounded possibility. For that realm is bereft, in Lovejoy's words, of 'any limiting and selective principle' (Lovejoy 1936: p. 331). The universe that has to be faced is one of potentially endless proliferation without check, balance or centre.

The problem of the lack of a centre lies at the heart of questions concerning the nature of Browning's identity in his poetry. It is well known that Browning was always unwilling to be identified directly as the speaker in his poems – including even lyric poems not explicitly defined as dramatic monologues. In a prefatory 'Advertisement' to his 1842 *Dramatic Lyrics* he described the poetry of that volume as 'for the most part Lyric in expression, always Dramatic in principle, and so many utterances of so many imaginary persons, not mine'. In 1868, in the Preface to his six volume *Poetical Works*, Browning re-emphasized the dramatic principle behind his work – not excluding *Pauline*, which had been subtitled *A Fragment of a Confession* without being designated (except perhaps in the fictitious name of the lady addressed) as spoken by someone other than the poet himself:

> The thing [*Pauline*] was my earliest attempt at 'poetry always dramatic in principle, and so many utterances of so many imaginary persons, not mine,' which I have since written according to a scheme less extravagant and scale less impracticable than ventured upon in this crude preliminary sketch . . .

Browning's attempts to dissociate himself from standard ideas of self-expression in poetry may be linked to that failure of confidence in Romantic idealist conceptions of the individual imagination which, as we have seen, is manifested in his poetry. High Romanticism had celebrated the individual imagination's activity in an active universe while seeking to limit the anarchic potential of that activity by referring its origin and ground to a transcendent spiritual zone. The centredness and coherence of the high Romantic 'I' was bought at the price of the contradictory claim that it stood both in and out of time. But the way that Browning's poetry concerns itself with the difficulty of making that claim means that while there are many characters in the poetry who themselves strive to make it – from Paracelsus' 'There is an inmost centre in us all, / Where truth abides in fulness' to Ben Ezra's 'Earth changes, but thy soul and God stand sure' – the verse itself is not founded on the claim. It persistently refuses to centre on and derive authority from its maker's voice. Where a voice such as that of the third speaker of the 'Epilogue' to *Dramatis Personae* seems close to articulating an authorially endorsed perspective, what it articulates is something that again calls in question the monolithic, authoritative 'I' of high Romanticism. For in the 'one world' advanced by that speaker, the creative imagination, however sacramentalized, loses absolute authority precisely through the exclusion of the external, transcendental dimension offered by a metaphysical dualism. The face of the sacred is not constant through time, but is decomposed to be recomposed.

What is also lost through the temporalization and internalization of the divine is any 'limiting and selective principle' within the human creative imagination. Within 'one world' the daemonic imagination may realize itself according to an unlimited range of possibilities. Without the absolute, objective point of reference claimed for subjectivity in Romantic ideology, the stability and unity of the subject cannot be maintained. Thus it is that Browning's poetry is so preoccupied from the start with the fragmentation of the single self. Isobel Armstrong has spoken of *Pauline*, with its speaker's striations of consciousness and voice, as 'discovering . . . the imagery of schizophrenia' (Armstrong 1969: p. 296). The range of Browning's implicitly or explicitly dramatic voices betrays as a whole his engagement with the possibility of a proliferation of selves. And, individually, some of the voices in Browning's verse speak very much more darkly than others about the implications of an ultimately unregulated potential for the creative imagination.

Take, for example, the Duke in Browning's *Dramatic Lyrics* monologue 'My Last Duchess'. It is a commonplace that, as the widowed Duke expounds upon the painting of his dead wife, we are being shown the kind of mind where a connoisseur's taste for art involves an atrophy of living human sympathy. But what is most important is that the aesthetic principle which directs the Duke's view of his last Duchess may be compared with the principle that directs, say, Fra Lippo's framing of reality or Caliban's construction of meaning in the universe. We discover that, in life, the Duchess had refused to conform to the Duke's picture of what she and, by extension, the world in general should be. And for that refusal he did finally, literally, 'frame' her. Her portrait may mock him now, frustrating him with the reminder that there are realities which escape the ordering powers of his own mind and will. But for all that he is teased, he still seeks to project his own fixed patterns on the world. The Duke's imagination constitutes a parody of the Romantic insistence that the individual imagination bears a total authority. There is a similar issue at stake in another monologue from *Dramatic Lyrics*, 'Porphyria's Lover'. Here the lover–speaker is committed to imposing his subjectivity on his loved-one, to constructing the other according to the terms of his gaze so that she ceases to exist as an autonomous being. But whatever the horror of the speaker's actual strangulation of Porphyria, a further dread of the poem appears at *its* end, as the lover sits with the body of the one he has murdered: 'all night long we have not stirred, / And yet God has not said a word' (ll. 59–60). The anxiety stirred by these lines is that there may be no God outside the speaker's imagination *to* say a word. Both the Duke and Porphyria's lover are types of the shaping imagination in action. But these poems no longer assert a transcendent limiting and selective principle which guarantees the positive nature of the imagination's operations. The disturbing potential latent in Romantic sacramentalization of subjectivity is exposed as these speakers shape the world in their own images. And not only, of course, the world in general. There is a preoccupation in these poems specifically with issues of gender and with the ways in which men may seek to usurp the imaginative autonomy of women (for a related, though varying, treatment of such matters see Browning's remarkable little poem from *Dramatis Personae*, 'A Likeness'). As Fra Lippo paints and repaints himself into existence he may decide that the world 'means good' (l. 314). But against that conviction must be placed the proclivities of other kinds of artist.

The point about an unregulatable proliferation of imaginative possibility applies equally, of course, to Browning the poet who imagines the imaginings. When Browning spoke of his poetry as the 'utterances of so many imaginary persons, not mine', the 'not mine' of that formulation preserved the notion of a Browning voice separate from the voices in his poetry. But the inclusion under 'imaginary persons' of lyric voices not explicitly designated as those of others than the poet throws the coherence of the 'not mine' – insofar as it relates to Browning's poetry – into doubt. For that inclusiveness – the insistence on the dramatic principle of *all* his verse – would mean that Browning has no poetic voice of his own at all. As has been suggested, Browning's unwillingness to be situated as the univocal speaker of his own verse, his groping towards a critical formulation of his non-presence in his poetry, relates to a failure of confidence in Romantic conceptions of the individual imagination and reveals a radical dubiety about his own authority as a centred and coherent 'I'. Yet this abdication of the transcendental poetic ego carries with it a different kind of authorial identification with the poetry. Browning *is* imaginatively implied in all the voices of his poetry, but he is implied *as* those voices, not as a unitary, self-sufficient identity which exists outside them and which can yet on occasion be distinguished speaking in all its integrity within some of them. It is not simply that Browning the author evacuates his lyrical verse, but that there is no single, distinct authorial reality to do such evacuating. In imagining a multiplicity of imaginings Browning coincides with that multiplicity.

This is a matter which affects crucially the question of judgement in Browning's dramatic monologues. Standard accounts may add several elements to the basic definition of the dramatic monologue as a first person poem spoken by someone who is indicated not to be the poet. M. H. Abrams, for example, notes that the dramatic occasion assumed in such monologues means that the person speaking will often utter their words 'in a specific situation at a critical moment' and that often 'this person addresses and interacts with one or more other people; but we know of the auditors' presence and what they say and do only from clues in the discourse of the single speaker'.[3] There may also be the notion that the very nature of the first person voice of a dramatic monologue draws us into a degree of sympathy with that voice. But perhaps the most important further point made in standard accounts of the dramatic monologue is that the reader is put into a position – whatever his or her capacity to enter into the imagination of the speaker of the monologue – of having to judge that speaker. Thus Abrams observes that 'the principle controlling the selection and organization of what the speaker says is the unintentional revelation of his temperament and character'.[4] This is a principle noted by Alan Sinfield when he summarizes the idea that the dramatic monologue form involves 'an ironic discrepancy between the speaker's view of himself and a larger judgement which the poet implies and the reader must develop' (Sinfield 1977: p. 7).

In its simplest application, the idea of a larger judgement shared between poet and reader posits, unproblematically, a univocal Browning located outside the poetic text and the existence of universal grounds for both poet's and reader's judgements. But this may be a reductive view of the dramatic monologue – a view which turns the poetry into nothing more than a vehicle for safe moral parable. Just as Mrs Orr was frustrated in her attempts to 'extract' a 'definite moral' from '"Childe Roland"', so Browning's dramatic monologues as a whole resist the complacency which may inform notions concerning the 'larger judgement' of poet and reader. What gives works such as 'My Last Duchess' or 'Porphyria's Lover' their peculiar power to fascinate and to stimulate different readings of their moral meaning is precisely that a controlling authorial perspective has disappeared. In his absence from his poems as an authoritative 'I' or judge, Browning is himself implicated in the uncertainties of position and evaluation generated by the poems. And by the same token so are we as readers of the poems. We may judge Porphyria's lover or the Duke and seek to insist that this judgement is endorsed by Browning. But this would be a construction on our own terms of both the poem and Browning. The most disturbing question put by the verse is that in such construction or framing we may be engaged in the same order of structuring activity as Porphyria's lover or the Duke. The monologues force us back to consider the grounds of our own judgement – even our own identities. We may assert an absolute authority in our own selves that Browning, in writing the poetry, did not himself assert. Or we may decide that the deepest implication of the dispersal of Browning's identity throughout his poetic voices is that our own reading has no total, objective point of reference.

We may find, moreover, that the concept of sympathy and judgement as the two contrary poles of a reader's response to Browning's dramatic monologues begins to lose meaning as the distinction between the two terms begins to break down. In a standard reading of 'The Bishop Orders His Tomb at Saint Praxed's Church' from *Dramatic Romances and Lyrics*, for instance, we might say that it is possible to be drawn into some sympathy with the dying Bishop's situation while at the same time agreeing with Ruskin who observed in *Modern Painters* (IV, 1856) that 'there is so much told . . . in these lines, of the Renaissance spirit, – its worldliness, inconsistency, pride, hypocrisy, ignorance of itself . . .' (Cook and Wedderburn 1903–12: VI, p. 449). It is possible, in other words, to assume authoritative grounds for judging the Bishop. But there is another sense in which sympathy with the Bishop can be seen to put us as readers into a position that is comparable to his experience of himself and which raises questions about the truth claims embedded in our judgements of him. That is to say, we are presented in the poem with a man who has been used in life to ordering and framing things according to his own desire. It is the same ordering impulse that we witness as, on his death bed, he plans the construction (to be undertaken after he is gone) of his tomb. But that attempt to dictate terms upon the form of his tomb stands as an attempt to dictate terms upon the formless. He is, in fact, trying to order or frame death itself. Yet even as he does so he recognizes, struggles with, and is terrified at, the impossibility of the attempt. It is an impossibility dramatized in many of the details of the poem. For example, in the way the Bishop cannot help but keep re-imagining his tomb. As the unimaginable pressure of the formless weighs upon him he strives to establish in his mind's eye a single, permanent structure as a kind of defence or bulwark against that formlessness. But in the face of the formless he cannot hold to a fixture and he abjectly, absurdly, keeps changing the specification of the materials out of which his monument is to be composed: 'I shall fill my slab of basalt', l. 25; 'Did I say basalt . . . ? Black – / 'Twas ever antique-black I meant!', ll. 53–4; 'all of jasper, then! / . . . There's plenty jasper somewhere in the world', ll. 68, 72. But there may be neither basalt, antique black, nor jasper beyond the world. Neither may there be materials or form for the Bishop's identity itself. The Bishop's predicament is that he cannot arrive at a sense of what the self is in the context of death, in the 'context' of *after*-life. The ordering powers of his mind have no purchase on the infinite. There is no absolute point of reference for his shaping imagination. Constituted and bound in time and space it can only project onto the infinite the terms of time and space. But the more he projects earthly orders onto death, the more the contingency and relativity of such orders are exposed. The more he piles up his orderings the faster the constituent elements slip and fail.

The process is enacted in the movement of the verse itself, where the syntax and rhythm of the lines search for a final command and closure that, by their own nature as contingent structures, they can never achieve. The movements of the Bishop's mind follow something like the logic of a nightmare, searching out a stability of position that is forever denied. On the 'edge of non-existence', finding no absolute guarantee of humanly recognizable pattern, edging towards a space 'where meaning collapses', the Bishop is on the 'edge of . . . hallucination' (Kristeva 1982: p. 2):

> Stone –
> Gritstone, a-crumble! Clammy squares which sweat
> As if the corpse they keep were oozing through –
> And no more *lapis* to delight the world!

> (115–18)

'The corpse', Julia Kristeva has observed, 'seen without God and outside of science',

> is the utmost of abjection. It is death infecting life. Abject. . . . It is . . . not lack of cleanliness or health that causes abjection but what disturbs identity, system, order. What does not respect borders, positions, rules.

> (Kristeva 1982: p. 4)

Threatening to erase distinction and difference the infinite, in 'The Bishop Orders His Tomb at Saint Praxed's Church', is about to invade and empty human order of content. And our sympathy with the Bishop may be more than an indulgence in the characteristics of a particular individual. It may be an unavoidable identification with this figure as a type of the general human relationship with that which lies outwith time and space, form and language, difference and individuality. The question of our judgement of the Bishop may be inextricable from that identification. For our attempts to form a judgement of the Bishop, to frame him within a context of meaning, may be as empty of absolute authority as the Bishop's own attempts to frame death. We might wish to think we can stand at a distance and indulge ourselves in contempt or pity for the Bishop. But at a deeper level, in facing the Bishop's desperation, we may be facing ourselves.

Desperation, however, is by itself too limited and limiting a word to describe the general tenor of Browning's studies in the human activity of formulating structures that may have no ultimate meaning. The speaker of '"Childe Roland to the Dark Tower Came"', for example, moves to a final moment of self-formulation and self-affirmation that is poised on an awareness that such formulation and affirmation may be void. It is a moment that epitomizes the special effect of Browning's overall poetic vision. For as Harold Bloom has commented, the distinctive feature of '"Childe Roland"' is the 'extraordinary, negative intensity of Childe Roland's consciousness, which brings to defeat an energy of perception so exuberant as to mock defeat's limits' (Bloom 1971: p. 162):

> There they stood, ranged along the hill-sides, met
>> To view the last of me, a living frame
>> For one more picture! in a sheet of flame
> I saw them and I knew them all. And yet
> Dauntless the slug-horn to my lips I set,
>> And blew, '*Childe Roland to the Dark Tower came,*'
>>>> (XXXIV)

NOTES TO THE CRITICAL COMMENTARY

1 See, for example, Milton, *Paradise Lost*: 'man . . . / . . . will fall, / . . . whose fault? / Whose but his own?' (III. 93, 95–7); 'Forth reaching to the fruit, she plucked, she ate: / Earth felt the wound' (IX, 781–2).

2 The Higher Criticism, associated in the nineteenth century especially with German scholarship, distinguished itself from the dogmatic use of Scripture by its critical inquiry into the human origins and historical circumstances of composition of the texts of the Bible. There were different emphases within nineteenth-century Higher Criticism (some committed to examining historical and textual data, some more speculative in character) but its broad demythologizing temper was opposed by those Christians who held to the traditional view that the New Testament was divinely inspired and the infallible revelation of true religion. Browning was familiar with the work of one of the most notable figures on the Higher Critical side, D. F. Strauss, whose *Leben Jesu* created something of a sensation when it appeared in 1835–6; as well as with Ernest Renan's

1863 *La Vie de Jésus* (see notes to the 'Epilogue' to *Dramatis Personae*). In 'A Death in the Desert' Browning uses the character of St John to dramatize some of the issues at stake in nineteenth-century debates about the Higher Criticism (see Elinor Shaffer, 'Browning's St John: The Casuistry of the Higher Criticism', *Victorian Studies*, 16, 1972, pp. 205–21). In the context of 'Caliban Upon Setebos', natural theology may be taken as the argument that the nature of God – far from being a matter of the revelation, in contravention of the laws of nature, of transcendent truth – is something that may be inferred 'scientifically' from evidences of design in the natural world (an argument that had been promulgated, for example, in the *Bridgewater Treatises (On the Power, Wisdom, and Goodness of God, as manifested in the Creation)*, 1833–40).

3 M. H. Abrams, *A Glossary of Literary Terms*, 4th edition, New York, Holt, Rinehart and Winston, 1981, p. 45.

4 ibid., p. 45.

Bibliography

This lists books and articles identified by short reference in the Introduction, Critical Commentary, and Notes, together with a selection of other works on or relating to Browning. Journals which carry essays on Browning include *Browning Society Notes*, *Browning Institute Studies*, *Studies in Browning and His Circle*, *Victorian Poetry* and *Victorian Studies*.

TEXTS

Altick, R. D. (ed.) (1971) *Robert Browning. The Ring and the Book*, Penguin English Poets Series, Harmondsworth, Penguin Books.

Brett-Smith, H. F. B. (ed.) (1921) *Peacock's 'Four Ages of Poetry'*, *Shelley's 'Defence of Poetry'*, *Browning's 'Essay on Shelley'*, Oxford, Basil Blackwell.

Browning, Robert (1888–9) *The Poetical Works of Robert Browning*, 16 volumes, London, Smith, Elder. The last collected edition seen through the press by the poet. Before his death Browning revised the first ten volumes of the first printing of the edition (see Kelley and Peterson, 1973). A seventeenth volume, incorporating *Asolando* (published on 12 December 1889, the day of Browning's death), appeared in 1894.

Jack, Ian (ed.) (1970) *Browning, Poetical Works 1833–1864*, Oxford Standard Authors, Oxford, Oxford University Press.

—— and Smith, Margaret (eds) (1983–4) *The Poetical Works of Robert Browning*, volumes I and II, Oxford, Clarendon Press.

—— and Fowler, Rowena (eds) (1988) *The Poetical Works of Robert Browning*, volume III, Oxford, Clarendon Press. This scholarly edition is still in progress.

Kelley, Philip and Peterson, W. S. (1973) 'Browning's Final Revisions', *Browning Institute Studies*, I. pp. 87–118.

Pettigrew, J. and Collins, T. J. (eds) (1981) *Robert Browning. The Poems*, 2 volumes, Penguin English Poets Series, Harmondsworth, Penguin Books. These volumes complement R. D. Altick's Penguin English Poets edition of *The Ring and the Book* and to date are the best readily available complete edition.

Pinion, F. B. (ed.) (1969) *Robert Browning. Dramatis Personae*, London and Glasgow, Collins.

Turner, Paul (ed.) (1972) *Browning, Men and Women*, Oxford, Oxford University Press.

A complete edition of Browning's poetry in the valuable Longman Annotated English Poets Series is currently in preparation, edited by Daniel Karlin and John Woolford.

BIOGRAPHY AND LETTERS

Curle, Richard (ed.) (1937) *Robert Browning and Julia Wedgewood: A Broken Friendship as Revealed by their Letters*, London, John Murray and Jonathan Cape.

DeVane, William Clyde and Knickerbocker, K. L. (eds) (1950) *New Letters of Robert Browning*, New Haven, Yale University Press.

Griffin, W. H. and Minchen, H. C. (1938) *The Life of Robert Browning*, revised edition, London, Macmillan (first published 1910).

Hood, Thurman (ed.) (1933) *Letters of Robert Browning, Collected by T. J. Wise*, New Haven, Yale University Press.

Hudson, R. and Kelley, P. (eds) (1984) *The Brownings' Correspondence*, volumes I and II, The first two volumes of a projected complete edition of the Brownings' correspondence.

Irvine, William and Honan, Park (1975) *The Book, the Ring, and the Poet. A Biography of Robert Browning*, London, Bodley Head.

Karlin, Daniel (1985) *The Courtship of Robert Browning and Elizabeth Barrett*, Oxford, Oxford University Press.

Karlin, Daniel (1989) *Robert Browning and Elizabeth Barrett. The Courtship Correspondence. A Selection*, Oxford, Clarendon Press.

Kenyon, Frederic G. (ed.) (1897) *The Letters of Elizabeth Barrett Browning*, 2 volumes, London, Smith, Elder.

Kintner, Elvan (ed.) (1969) *The Letters of Robert Browning and Elizabeth Barrett Browning, 1845–1846*, 2 volumes, Cambridge, Ma., Belknap Press, Harvard University Press.

CRITICISM AND CONTEXTS

Armstrong, Isobel (1969) 'The Brownings', in Arthur Pollard (ed.) *Sphere History of Literature in the English Language, Volume 6, The Victorians*, London, Sphere Books.

—— (ed.) (1969a) *The Major Victorian Poets: Reconsiderations*, London, Routledge and Kegan Paul.

—— (ed.) (1972) *Victorian Scrutinies, Reviews of Poetry 1830 to 1870*, London, Athlone Press.

—— (ed.) (1974) *Writers and their Background, Robert Browning*, London, G. Bell and Sons.

Ball, Patricia (1965) 'Browning's Godot', in *Victorian Poetry*, 3, pp. 245–53.

Belsey, Catherine (1986) 'The Romantic Construction of the Unconscious', in Francis Barker et al., (eds) *Literature, Politics and Theory, Papers from the Essex Conference 1976–84*, London and New York, Methuen.

Biswas, Robindra Kumar (1972) *Arthur Hugh Clough. Towards a Reconsideration*, Oxford, Clarendon Press.

Bloom, Harold (1971) *The Ringers in the Tower, Studies in Romantic Tradition*, Chicago and London, University of Chicago Press.

—— (1976) *Poetry and Repression: Revisionism from Blake to Stevens*, New Haven, Yale University Press.

—— and Munich, Adrienne (eds) (1979) *Robert Browning. A Collection of Critical Essays*, Twentieth Century Views Series, Englewood Cliffs, NJ, Prentice-Hall.

Cook, E. T. and Wedderburn, A. (eds) (1903–12) *The Works of John Ruskin*, Library Edition, 39 volumes, London, George Allen.

DeVane, William Clyde (1955) *A Browning Handbook*, 2nd edi-

184

tion, New York, Appleton–Century–Crofts (first published 1935).

Drew, Philip (ed.) (1966) *Robert Browning. A Collection of Critical Essays*, London, Methuen.

Griffiths, Eric (1989) *The Printed Voice of Victorian Poetry*, Oxford, Clarendon Press.

Miller, J. Hillis (1963) *The Disappearance of God: Five Nineteenth-Century Writers*, Cambridge, Ma., Harvard University Press.

Hulme, T. E. (1924) 'Romanticism and Classicism', *Speculations. Essays on Humanism and the Philosophy of Art*, London, Kegan Paul.

Kristeva, Julia (1982) *Powers of Horror, An Essay on Abjection*, translated by Leon S. Roudiez, New York, Columbia University Press (first published 1980).

Litzinger, Boyd and Knickerbocker, K. L. (eds) (1965) *The Browning Critics*, Lexington, University Press of Kentucky.

—— and Smalley, Donald (eds) (1970) *Browning. The Critical Heritage*, London, Routledge and Kegan Paul.

Lovejoy, Arthur O. (1936) *The Great Chain of Being, A Study of the History of an Idea*, Cambridge, Ma., Harvard University Press.

Martin, Loy D. (1985) *Browning's Dramatic Monologues and the Post-Romantic Subject*, Baltimore, Johns Hopkins University Press.

Orr, Mrs Sutherland (1896) *A Handbook to the Works of Robert Browning*, 7th edition, London, George Bell (first published 1884).

Shaw, W. David (1968) *The Dialectical Temper: The Rhetorical Art of Robert Browning*, Ithaca, NY, Cornell University Press.

Sinfield, Alan (1977) *Dramatic Monologue*, London, Methuen.

Tucker, Herbert F. (1980) *Browning's Beginnings, The Art of Disclosure*, Minneapolis, University of Minnesota Press.

Vasari, Giorgio (1987) *Lives of the Artists*, a selection translated by George Bull, 2 volumes, Harmondsworth, Penguin. Vasari's *Lives of the Most Excellent Painters, Sculptors, and Architects* was first published in 1550, followed by a revised and enlarged second edition in 1568.

Notes

The following abbreviations are used in the notes.

1842   *Dramatic Lyrics*
1845   *Dramatic Romances and Lyrics*
1849   *Poems* (2 volumes)
1855   *Men and Women*
1863   *The Poetical Works* (3 volumes)
1864   *Dramatis Personae*

Vasari   *Lives of the Artists* by Giorgio Vasari (Vasari, 1987)

The notes to each poem include, first, brief details of composition and publication; second, a summary of the subject and sources of the poem; third, information on specific references, allusions, etc., in the text. Indication is given where there is further discussion of a poem in the Introduction and/or Critical Commentary.

MY LAST DUCHESS. FERRRA

Written summer or early autumn 1842. First published *1842* where the poem was entitled 'I. – Italy' and paired, under the general caption 'Italy and France', with a piece entitled 'II. – France' (now 'Count Gismond. Aix in Provence'). The poems, no longer linked by a general caption, appeared under their present titles in *1849*.

'A widowed Duke of Ferrara is exhibiting the portrait of his former wife, to the envoy of some nobleman whose daughter he proposes to marry' (Orr 1896: p. 250). The Duke was suggested by Alfonso II (1533–97), fifth Duke of Ferrara, patron of the arts and the last of the ancient and powerful Este family. In 1558 Alfonso married the 14-year-old Lucrezia de' Medici; Lucrezia died in 1561 and there was suspicion she had been poisoned. In 1565 the Duke married the daughter of Ferdinand, Count of Tyrol, whose capital was Innsbruck; the arrangements for the marriage having been conducted by an envoy. Browning's Duke is aristocratically egotistical, his aestheticism a cruelly refined form of materialism. Discussion of the poem has centred on why the Duke betrays so much – his disdain for and jealousy of his dead wife, along with a hint that he ordered her to be disposed of – to the envoy representing the family of his prospective wife. See Critical Commentary, pp. 174–5.

3	*Frà Pandolf* Brother Pandolf, apparently an imaginary painter from a monastic order.
6–12	*never read . . . glance came there* the Duke explains that visitors in the past, seeing or reading a particular expression in the painted face of the Duchess, had always seemed as if about to ask the Duke what the cause of the expression was. The passage introduces the element of specifically sexual jealousy which pervades the Duke's sense of his former wife.
25	*favour* a ribbon or some other gift received and worn as a token of love.
32–4	*as if she ranked . . . anybody's gift* the rankling pride of the ancient aristocracy is a theme also in *The Ring and the Book*. In terms of Browning's historical models, the Estes would have regarded the Medici as *nouveaux riches*.
45	*I gave commands* the nature of these commands is left insinuatingly vague. Hiram Corson (*An Introduction to the Study of Robert Browning's Poetry*, 3rd edition, Boston, Heath, 1903, p. viii) reported Browning as saying: 'the commands were that she should be put to death. . . . Or he might have had her shut up in a convent'.

54–6   *Neptune . . . sea-horse . . . Claus of Innsbruck*   the Duke
        refers to a sculpture of the Roman sea god subduing a
        mythical beast, half horse and half fish. Claus of
        Innsbruck is apparently an imaginary artist. The Duke's
        glancingly appreciative reference to the sculpture, fol-
        lowing his meditation upon the 'wonder' (1.3) that is
        the painting of his former wife, confirms his inhuman
        connoisseurship. The reference may include an indirect
        compliment to Ferdinand of Innsbruck (see headnote).
        There is also a threatening connotation – in the particu-
        lar scene portrayed by the sculpture – of that impulse
        towards psycho-sexual domination which has been a
        theme throughout the poem.

SOLILOQUY OF THE SPANISH CLOISTER

Date of composition unknown. First published *1842*, where it
was titled 'II. – Cloister. (*Spanish*)' and paired, under the general
heading 'Camp and Cloister', with a work titled 'I. – Camp.
(*French*)' (now 'Incident of the French Camp'). The poems
appeared independently under their present titles in *1849*.

'[A] venemous outbreak of jealous hatred, directed by one monk
against another' (Orr 1896: p. 251). The speaker's disturbed state
of mind does not necessarily invalidate everything that he has to
say about the speciousness of Brother Lawrence's virtue.

10   *Salve tibi!*   'Hail to you!' (Latin).
14   *oak-galls*   swellings on diseased oak-leaves, yielding
      tannin (used in dyeing, etc.).
16   *Swine's Snout*   translation of the Latin – *rostrum porci-
      num* – for dandelion.
22   *chaps*   chops: jaws, mouth.
24   *lily*   symbol of purity in Christian art. A likely insinua-
      tion is that Lawrence's apparent holiness is contradicted
      by the egotism of inscribing his initial (1. 23). In the next
      stanza the speaker will impute Lawrence with a secret
      lust for convent nuns.
31   *Barbary corsair*   pirate of the Barbary coast of north-
      west Africa.

33	*refection* meal.
39	*Arian* follower of the fourth-century heretic Arius, who rejected the orthodox doctrine of the Trinity and of Christ's equality with God the Father.
49–51	*great text . . . damnations* There is no such text in Galatians, though there is a link between a passage in Galatians (3:10) and the Old Testament book of law, Deuteronomy, in which are written twenty-nine verses (28: 16–44) enumerating curses against the disobedient. Browning may have been conflating a memory of Galatians with one of Deuteronomy. In a letter of 1888 he wrote that a 'lapse of memory would seem to occur in the case of the Text from Galatians, but I was not careful to be correct' (see David George, *Studies in Browning and His Circle*, 2, 1974: p. 62). Sometimes, of course, Browning had his speakers make mistakes as part of his characterization of them.
56	*Manichee* a follower of Manichaeism, an heretical system of belief developed in the third century which held that the universe is caught in a war between equally balanced forces of good and evil. The speaker fantasizes that he may be able – in a complicated theological argument – to trick Brother Lawrence into taking up an heretical position for which, if he had not time to recant, he would be damned. In the final stanza the speaker will imagine that by pretending to sell his soul to Satan he can trick Satan himself into destroying Brother Lawrence's rose-acacia tree!
60	*Belial's gripe* the grip of one of the princes of darkness.
64	*sieve* type of container, with perforations.
70	*Hy, Zy, Hine* three much puzzled-over words. Perhaps a fragment of a magic incantation used to seal a pact with the devil, they probably have no rational meaning (see J. F. Loucks, *Victorian Poetry*, 12, 1974: pp. 165–9).
71	*Vespers* evening prayer.
71–2	*Plena . . . Virgo* 'Full of grace, Hail, Virgin' (Latin). The confusion of the normal religious formulation ('Ave Maria, gratia plena') may be intended as a symptom of the speaker's disordered state of mind.

Probably composed 1835. First published as 'Johannes Agricola' in the *Monthly Repository* for January 1836, together with 'Porphyria' (now 'Porphyria's Lover'). In *1842* neither poem was individually titled, both appearing under the general heading 'Madhouse Cells' with 'Johannes Agricola' simply numbered 'I' and the other 'II'. In *1849* the poems appeared as 'I. – Madhouse Cell./Johannes Agricola in Meditation' and 'II. – Madhouse Cell. / Porphyria's Lover'. The 'Madhouse Cell' headings (and linking between the two poems) were dropped in *1863*.

Johannes Agricola (1494–1566), the speaker of this monologue, was a German protestant extremist (born Schnitter or Schneider) who founded Antinomianism, an heretical doctrine which held, in broad terms, that the moral law is not binding upon Christians who, under the law of divine grace, are 'elect'; that is, predestined to be saved. Browning appended a headnote defining the doctrine when he published the poem in the *Monthly Repository*:

> 'Antinomians, so denominated for rejecting the Law as a thing of no use under the Gospel dispensation: they say, that good works do not further, nor evil works hinder salvation; that the child of God cannot sin . . . that the child of grace being once assured of salvation, afterwards never doubteth. . . . '—*Dictionary of all Religions*, 1704.

For a study of perverted religious thought and feeling, compare Tennyson's dramatic monologue 'St Simeon Stylites' (1842).

11	*I lie . . . always lain* As one predestined to be saved, Agricola considers himself, even though he is caught up in the fallen human and natural world, never to have been alienated from the spiritual presence of God.
32	*poison-gourd* a figure of the damned. The corollary of the idea that some of God's creatures are predestined – whatever they do in life – to be saved, is that some are predetermined to be damned.
60	*right hand* token of election and exaltation, of divine approval and favour (see Matthew 25:34).

PORPHYRIA'S LOVER

Probably composed 1835. For publication details, see notes to 'Johannes Agricola in Meditation' above.

The monologue is spoken by Porphyria's lover on the night he has murdered her. Some of the details in this study of psychosis were suggested by B. W. Procter's poem 'Marcian Colonna' (1820) and by a passage written by John Wilson in *Blackwood's Magazine* (1818) – 'Extracts from Gosschen's Diary' (see M. Mason in Armstrong 1974: pp. 255–8). See Critical Commentary, p. 175.

HOME-THOUGHTS, FROM ABROAD

Date of composition unknown. First published *1845*, where it formed the first part of a three-part poem (neither of the other two parts had a different title). In *1849* this poem was separated from 'Home-Thoughts, from the Sea' (the third part of *1845*) and 'Here's to Nelson's Memory'.

THE BISHOP ORDERS HIS TOMB AT SAINT PRAXED'S CHURCH

Date of composition usually ascribed to the winter of 1844–5, but possibly written earlier. Published as 'The Tomb at Saint Praxed's' in *Hood's Magazine* for March 1845, before inclusion in *1845*. The present title was adopted in *1849*.

'The Bishop is at the point of death. His sons (nominally nephews) are about him; and he is urging on them anxious and minute directions for the tomb they are to place for him in St Praxed's church' (Orr 1896: p. 246). The Bishop is presented as a type of Renaissance prelate rather than as a specific historical figure. St Praxed's Church (the Basilica of Santa Prassede, after a second-century virgin saint famed for giving her wealth to the poor) is in Rome, but differs architecturally in several respects from the one imaged in the poem and has no tomb corresponding to that projected by Browning's Bishop. In *Modern Painters* (IV, 1856) Ruskin observed of the work: 'I know of no other piece of modern English . . . in which there is so much told . . . of the

Renaissance spirit, – its worldliness, inconsistency, pride, hypocrisy, ignorance of itself, love of art, of luxury, and of good Latin' (Cook and Wedderburn 1903–12: VI, p. 449). See Critical Commentary, pp. 177–9.

1	*Vanity . . . vanity* 'Vanity of vanities, saith the Preacher, vanity of vanities; all is vanity' (Ecclesiastes 1:2).
2	*Anselm* one of the Bishop's illegitimate sons – euphemistically referred to in the succeeding line as 'Nephews'.
5	*Gandolf* the Bishop's archrival in love as in other matters, now dead; like the other personages in the poem, he is fictitious.
17	*cozened* tricked or defrauded. According to the Bishop, the site ('niche', l. 16) of Gandolf's family tomb within the church was gained by deception from the Bishop himself.
21	*epistle-side* the right side (as one faces the altar) from where the Epistle is read during Mass. Denied his preferred site for a tomb, the Bishop attempts to make the best of the situation and imagines the view of the church interior from the position he is left with.
25	*basalt* greenish- or brownish-black rock, frequently used as tomb stone.
26	*tabernacle* canopy over a tomb.
28	*The odd one . . . where Anselm stands* as the Bishop imagines how he will lie, when dead, within the structure of his tomb he blends that image with his present position on his death-bed surrounded by his sons.
30	*pulse* pulp of the grape. The word also touches those connotations of sensuous life-force, of heart-beat and life-blood, that ironically suffuse the Bishop's imaginings of death throughout the poem.
31	*onion-stone* inferior marble liable to flake off in layers.
34	*conflagration* the Bishop here shifts momentarily into remembering a fire which once damaged the church.
39	*Ah God, I know not, I!* As the following lines make clear, the Bishop retrieved a lump of precious stone from the fire-damaged church and secreted it in an

oil-press (l. 37). The expostulation here may be an expression of the Bishop's automatic impulse to evade responsibility for a wrong-doing.

41 *frail* basket.

42 *lapis lazuli* semi-precious blue stone.

46 *Frascati* beautiful resort town near Rome.

49 *Jesu Church* The sixteenth-century Chiesa del Gesù in Rome has a seventeenth-century altar showing the Trinity with an angel holding a large globe of lapis lazuli.

51 *Swift . . . years* 'My days are swifter than a weaver's shuttle, and are spent without hope' (Job 7: 6)

52 *Man goeth . . . where is he?* 'he that goeth down to the grave shall come up no more' (Job 7: 9); ' man giveth up the ghost, and where is he?' (Job 14: 10).

54 *antique-black* black stone more handsome and costly than basalt.

55 *frieze* a band of painted or sculptured decoration.

56 *bas-relief* sculpture in low relief.

57 *Pans* Pan, Greek god of fields and forests: by the Renaissance an impersonation of Nature; often associated with sexual licence.
    Nymphs minor deities, beautiful maidens. The Bishop's desire to have such classical figures on his Christian tomb emphasizes the confusion in his mind between the sensuous and worldly, on one hand, and the spiritual, on the other.
    wot know (archaism).

58 *tripod* stool associated with the oracles of Apollo at Delphi.
    thyrsus ornamented staff of Dionysus (Bacchus), god of wine and fertility, associated with orgiastic rites.

60 *glory* halo.

62 *tables* tablets of stone – on which were written the Commandments (Exodus 24–36).

65 *revel down* enjoy, dissipate my wealth.

66 *travertine* limestone, which the Bishop fears his sons will use to complete his tomb instead of the costly materials he is ordering.

68 *jasper* a translucent green quartz.

70	*bath* large, luxurious pool.
77	*Tully's* Marcus Tullius Cicero (106–43 BC), Roman master of rhetoric, often considered the purest Latin stylist.
79	*Ulpian* Domitius Ulpianus (170–228), a Roman jurist, whose prose style represents a debasement of the classical purity associated with Cicero. The Bishop is priding himself on the fact that an Ulpian Latin has been used on Gandolf's tomb.
82	*God made and eaten* a reference to the doctrine of transubstantiation. The crudeness of the Bishop's reference again emphasizes the carnality of his imagination.
87	*crook* Bishop's crozier.
89	*mortcloth* funeral pall.
95	*Saint Praxed . . . mount* compare l. 59. The Bishop here confuses the female St Praxed with Christ.
99	*ELUCESCEBAT* 'He was illustrious', an example of Ulpian Latin (Ciceronian Latin would be *elucebat*): this is the inscription on Gandolf's tomb (see l. 77n and l. 79n) and the following line (100) makes clear that it was the Bishop who had ordered the statement to be written in inferior Latin.
101	*Evil . . . pilgrimage* 'The days of the years of my pilgrimage are an hundred and thirty years: few and evil have the days of the years of my life been' (Genesis 47:9).
108	*vizor* mask of a helmet.
	Term bust on a pedestal, of the kind erected to honour Terminus, Roman god of boundaries.
109	*lynx* Dionysus is frequently represented as attended by lynxes.
111	*entablature* the structure supporting the dead body and the state of being laid out.
116	*Gritstone* cheap/coarse sandstone.

LOVE AMONG THE RUINS

Probably written 1852 or 1853, but the date remains uncertain. First published as the opening poem of *1855*.

Picturing two young lovers meeting in a rural landscape which is the site of a once great imperial city, the scenery of the poem was suggested in part by the countryside around Rome and in part by accounts – such as A. H. Layard's *Nineveh and its Remains* (1849) – of ancient ruined cities (see J. Parr, *Publications of the Modern Language Association*, 68, 1953: pp. 128–37). The poem contrasts a martial culture based on simple values and certainties with the modern lovers who exist in a world where such values and certainties have long since disappeared, been ruined. The limitations of the martial culture are hinted at in allusions such as those to 'Lust' (l. 33) and the 'gold' that 'Bought and sold' both 'glory' and 'shame' (ll. 35–6). But the affirmation of the situation of the modern lovers at the end of the poem is qualified by the implicit recognition that they have only themselves and no absolute cultural values to rely on; that they do not, in fact, inhabit some pastoral idyll but a world of uncertainty and ambiguity (dramatized in the contrast between the 'undistinguished grey', l. 53, of the contemporary landscape and the bold, primary colours associated with the civilization of the past). Compare 'Cleon'.

9	*its prince* [that] its prince.
21–4	*hundred-gated . . . Twelve abreast* Babylon and the Egyptian Thebes were said to have had a hundred gates, and Nineveh to have had walls on which three chariots might drive abreast.
30	*Stock* stump, support, foundation.
39	*caper* a trailing shrub.
41	*houseleek* a flowering plant often growing in walls and roofs.
65	*causeys* causeways.

FRA LIPPO LIPPI

Probably written 1853 in Florence; first published *1855*.

Supposed to be uttered by the painter–monk Fra Filippo Lippi (c. 1406–69), the monologue is set in Florence in the middle of the fifteenth century. The episode treated in the poem assumes that Lippo has been working at the palace of his patron, the Florentine ruler and patron of the arts Cosimo of the Medici (1389–1464), for whom he has been painting 'saints and saints / And saints again' (ll. 48–9). On the occasion pictured at the outset of the poem Lippo has left the confinements of his work ('I could not paint all night –', l. 49) to visit a district of the city that has a certain reputation ('sportive ladies', l. 6); returning from that district he has been apprehended and is in the process of being questioned by the night-watch. He proceeds to explain whom he is and to give an account of his life and work. Apart from Browning's familiarity with Lippo's paintings, the main source of the poem is the sketch in *Vasari*. See Critical Commentary, pp. 161–5.

3	*Zooks* abbreviation of the mild oath 'Gadzooks' (God's hooks) the meaning of which is not certain but can stand for something like 'By God'.
7	*Carmine* a Florentine monastery of the Carmelite order.
20	*gullet* throat or neck (oesophagus); i.e. 'how did you presume to grip the throat of a personage such as me?'
31–4	*I'd like his face . . . by the hair* In the same manner as he observes in l. 25 – 'He's Judas to a tittle, that man is!' – Lippo here declares that he would like to use one of the guard's faces as a model for his painting of the 'slave' who held John the Baptist's head after decapitation. Lippo's actual frescoes of John the Baptist are at Prato near Florence.
53–7	*Flower . . . thyme* Such 'whiffs' (l. 52) or snatches of song – recurring throughout Lippo's monologue – are meant to suggest *stornelli*, three-line Tuscan folk-songs beginning with a reference to a flower.
67	*Saint Laurence* the Florentine church of San Lorenzo.
73	*Jerome* ascetic saint (340–420), the subject of a painting by Lippo now in the Uffizi gallery, Florence.
75	*snap* seize.
81–2	*I was . . . in the street* Vasari says Lippo was orphaned at two years old and then for six years brought up by his aunt, Mona Lapaccia, before being put (see ll. 88–91) into the care of Carmelite Friars.
121	*the Eight* the magistrates of Florence.
130	*antiphonary* book with choral music.

196

139	*Camaldolese* a religious order with headquarters at Camaldoli, near Florence.
140	*Preaching Friars* the religious order of Dominicans.
148	*cribs* petty thefts.
170	*niece* probably a euphemism for mistress or daughter.
172	*funked* went out in smoke.
186	*In that shape . . . mouth* an ancient idea that the soul leaves the body as a vapour with the last breath.
189	*Giotto* Giotto di Bondone (c. 1266/7–1337), major Florentine artist whose paintings of St Francis are described in *Vasari*.
196–7	*Herodias . . . heads cut off* In Matthew 14:3–11 Salome danced for Herod and gained in payment the head of John the Baptist. Herodias was Salome's mother and the confusion of mother with daughter is perhaps designed to suggest that the Prior is ignorant even of one of the most famous stories in the Bible.
227	*Corner-house* the Medici palace, as in l. 18.
235–6	*Angelico . . . Lorenzo* Fra Angelico (c. 1400–55), outstanding painter of the school of Giotto; Lorenzo Monaco (c. 1370–c. 1425), master of Fra Angelico. The contrast is between the spiritually refined but highly formal religious painting of Fra Angelico and Lippo's insurgent naturalistic mode.
237	*Fag* toil.
250	*the cup runs over* 'my cup runneth over' (Psalm 23:5).
266	*the garden* Eden.
276	*Guidi* Tommaso Guidi (1401–28?), known as Masaccio (hulking, clumsy Thomas) because of his personal slovenliness. Browning turns Guidi into Lippo's pupil, when he was actually Lippo's teacher. The error arises from footnotes in Browning's Milanesi edition of *Vasari* (see J. Parr, *English Language Notes*, 3, 1966: pp. 197–201).
307	*cullion* rascal.
323	*Saint Laurence* a martyr-saint, roasted to death on a grid-iron (c.258).
327	*phiz* colloquially – physiognomy or face.
337	*wot* knows (archaism).
346	*Sant' Ambrogio's* Florentine convent for which Lippo

painted his *Coronation of the Virgin* (now in the Uffizi gallery), the work described by Lippo in the following lines.

347   *cast o' my office*   sample of my work.

351   *orris-root*   iris-root, sometimes used in making perfume.

354   *Saint John*   the Baptist, patron-saint of Florence.

358   *Uz*   Job's birthplace (Job 1:1).

364   *Mazed*   bewildered.

375   *camel-hair*   Saint John clothed himself with 'camel's hair' (Matthew 3:4; Mark 1:6).

377   *Iste . . . opus*   'This man ordered the work' (Latin). These words appear in a scroll in Lippo's *Coronation of the Virgin*; in Browning's day the figure they are associated with was thought to be Lippo, but is now understood to be Canon Maringhi who commissoned the altar-piece in 1441.

380   *kirtles*   skirts.

381   *hot cockles*   a rustic game; here a euphemism for sexual activity.

387   *Saint Lucy*   a virgin-martyr, put to death c. AD 304. The movement from the euphemistically-named Prior's *niece* to the figure of Saint Lucy captures in miniature the uneasy negotiation between the sensual and the spiritual which has run throughout the poem.

A TOCCATA OF GALUPPI'S

Date of composition unknown; first published *1855*.

The poem's speaker is an imaginary English person, an admirer of the Venetian composer Baldassare Galuppi (1706–85), best known for his light operas. A toccata (Italian, *toccare*, 'to touch') is a 'composition for a keyboard instrument, intended to exhibit the touch and technique of the performer, and having the air of an improvisation' (OED). In 1887 Browning wrote: 'As for Galuppi, I had once in my possession two huge manuscript volumes almost exclusively made up of his "Toccata-pieces" – apparently a slighter form of the Sonata to be "touched" lightly off' (see H. E. Greene, *Publications of the Modern Language Associa-*

tion, 62, 1947: p. 1099). It seems that it was the general character of Galuppi's keyboard composition, rather than any specific work, which Browning had in mind when writing the poem. The speaker of the poem, a Victorian who has never been to Italy, is partly censorious of what he takes to be a Venetian frivolity and gaiety represented in Galuppi's music. But he also recognizes graver tones beneath the surface of that music and in the last four stanzas he qualifies his own censoriousness as he has Galuppi mockingly point out that earnest Victorians die just as surely as Venetian revellers.

6   *Saint Mark's*   the cathedral of Venice.

         Doges . . . rings   in an annual ceremony the Doge or chief magistrate of Venice would cast a gold ring into the sea (a gesture of union, of 'wedding') to symbolize the Republic's maritime power.

8   *Shylock's bridge*   the Rialto, bridging Venice's Grand Canal (mentioned by Shakespeare's Shylock in *The Merchant of Venice*, I. iii. 102).

18   *clavichord*   stringed keyboard instrument, precursor of the modern piano.

19–21   *lesser thirds . . . commiserating sevenths*   a series of technical musical terms. Commonly thought to evoke moods of tenderness and grief, Browning characterizes the effect of lesser (minor) thirds as 'plaintive', in the same way as he then characterizes 'sixths diminished' (probably minor sixths) in terms of sighing. A suspension (l. 20) is a note held over from one chord to another, producing a temporary discord; the concordance (solution, l. 20) is achieved when the held-over note is resolved into a note appropriate to the new chord. The terms are used here to register a movement from anxiety at the thought of death to recognition that in the frame and order of things it is unavoidable. The commiseration of the 'sevenths' (mildly discordant notes) in l. 21 suggests, however, that there is no easy acceptance of death as the necessary 'resolution' of life.

24–5   *dominant's persistence . . . octave struck the answer*   In musical terms a 'dominant' is the fifth note above or the fourth below the tonic or key-note. It is 'the note in a mode or scale which, in traditional harmonic procedures, most urgently demands resolution upon the tonic' (*Grove's Dictionary of Music and Musicians*, 5th edition, ed. Eric Blom, London, Macmillan, 1954). Browning uses the musical notation of the dominant to suggest the awareness of mortality that persists through all the lighter or happier moods of life. The 'octave' (l. 25) – a perfect consonance – brings the resolution (the 'answer') demanded by the dominant. It finishes the musical piece in a state of exact form as death ends the dissonance (but also the variety) of life.

38   *rise in their degree* according to their appropriate position in the scale of creation.

43   *want* lack. From a partial disapproval the speaker has moved to intense sympathy with the passing of human beauty and happiness that is epitomized for him by Galuppi's Venice.

BY THE FIRE-SIDE

Usually thought to have been written late 1853, elements of the scenery having been suggested by a trip made by the Brownings in that year to Prato Fiorito, near Bagni di Lucca. But just possibly written as early as 1847, the scenery suggested by a description of Lake Orta, in Piedmont, given in a guide-book consulted by the Brownings (see J. S. Lindsay, *Studies in Philology*, 39, 1942: pp. 571–9). First published *1855*.

In this work a speaker, in something like middle-age, is found meditating on the past and his youth; he is at once engaged in projecting the manner in which he will remember his youth in the future, in old age. The poem 'is two accounts of the same memory or two overlapping memories of the same experience, built up by alternating a series of reveries in the present with the memories of the past. The situation is complicated by the fact that the speaker begins in the hypothetical future, imagining himself as an old man imagining the past (stanzas 1–5). Then follows an account of what is actually past, the autumn walk which he and his wife took as lovers to a deserted church in the Italian mountains. This account is interrupted and concluded by reverie spoken in the present (stanzas 21–30; 47–53)' (Armstrong 1969a: p. 105). 'By the Fire-Side' is often seen as one of Browning's more 'personal' poems, clearly related to his love for Elizabeth Barrett, who may be taken as a model for the portrait of 'Leonor'. But the work is a dramatic monologue, not literal autobiography.

16–25   *I shall be . . . green degrees*   Immersion in Greek leads to an opening up of mental – here primarily memorial – spaces that go far beyond the study of Greek itself ('I pass out where it ends', l. 20). The movement of the mind towards greater inwardness is dramatized as a progress through succeeding frames of reference – frames imaged as woven out of the branches of trees, with the hazels (ll. 14 and 21) mentioned by the 'young ones' (l. 11) at the start, followed by foreign trees ('a rarer sort', l. 23), which mark the speaker's passage into memories of his youth in Italy. From one point of view there is a narrowing of scope of reference ('outside-frame . . .', l. 21; 'inside-archway . . .', l. 22); but from another point of view such narrowing is at the same time a form of expanding horizons ('inside-archway widens fast').

27   *leader's hand*   perhaps wife's hand, in the sense that an image of her is an integral part of the speaker's memory.

43   *Pella*   settlement on Lake Orta.

64   *freaked*   streaked.

74   *fret*   eat into, erode.

77   *festa-day*   (Italian) 'feast' or religious holiday.

84   *wattled cote*   rough thatched shelter.

89   *John*   the Baptist, in the wilderness.

92   *pent-house*   projecting cover or roof.

95   *'Five, six, nine*   1569.

101   *Leonor*   the name of the faithful wife in Beethoven's opera *Fidelio*.

105   *The path . . . abhor*   'The process of recalling ["look backward", l. 103] and imaginatively reliving ["pursue", l. 104] past experience. Grey heads abhor it, because it confronts them with a sharp contrast between "flowery" [l. 107] youth and their present "waste" [l.

125] age. But the speaker dares to relive *his* life in memory because, thanks to his wife, his age seems "flowery" and his youth (before he met her) relatively "waste"' (Turner 1972: p. 323).

109–10   *the gulf . . . safe hem*   the point where youth passes ('drops') and beyond which it is felt that there remains no safe ground for life.

113–4   *great brow . . . propping it*   conventionally recognized as a characteristic pose of Elizabeth Barrett.

132   *great Word . . . new*   'And he that sat upon the throne said, Behold, I make all things new' (Revelation 21:5).

134   *change*   spiritual resurrection (see 1 Corinthians 15:51; 'We shall not all sleep, but we shall all be changed').

135   *house . . . hands*   2 Corinthians 5:1; 'we have a building of God, an house not made with hands, eternal in the heavens.'

171   *settle*   bench.

182   *stock*   log, stump.

185   *chrysolite*   green or yellow semi–precious stone.

186–7   *never a third . . . each by each*   The love letters between Browning and Elizabeth Barrett sometimes figure a 'third person', an imaginary outsider who objectively views their relationship (see Kintner 1969: I, pp. 178, 494–501). But see also the 'shadowy third' in l. 229; the reference here seems to contrast with that in l. 186. The 'one and one' of l. 229 is a figure of two lives having joined (see l. 228), whereas the 'each by each' of l. 187 is a token of a degree of separateness (see also the references to 'screen' in l. 196 and to 'guard between' in l. 198). The implication may be that where there is still some distance between lovers, each retains a conventional individuality; but when such distance has disappeared and the two lovers have fully united, then a kind of ghostly 'third' emerges which is the psychological vestige of the distinct individuality of these lovers whose two lives have in some sense merged.

245   *By its fruit*   'Ye shall know them by their fruits' (Matthew 7:16).

AN EPISTLE CONTAINING THE STRANGE MEDICAL EXPERIENCE
OF KARSHISH, THE ARAB PHYSICIAN

Date of composition unknown, but possibly 1853–4; first published *1855*.

Browning casts Karshish as an itinerant Arab physician who is writing to Abib, his master in the science of medicine. Both Karshish and Abib are fictitious. Set in Palestine in AD 66 or 69–70 the poem has Karshish telling of an encounter with Lazarus, who according to Gospel tradition (John 11:1–44) was raised from the dead by Christ. Karshish is torn between a sceptical 'scientific' view of the matter (speculating that Lazarus' reason has been impaired by a sudden awakening from what was no more than a prolonged epileptic trance), and a yearning to be able to believe in the substance of Lazarus' claim. See Critical Commentary, p. 166.

1–20	*Karshish . . . time* Karshish's elaborate opening to his twenty-second letter to Abib is in the manner of St Paul's Epistle to the Romans 1:1–7.
1	*Karshish* the name is derived from an Arabic word meaning 'one who gathers' or 'picks up'.
6	*puff of vapour* alluding to the ancient notion that the soul leaves the body at death in the form of a vapour.
12	*source* God or the world-soul. The poem does not present Karshish as a strict materialist but as holding a conception of the spiritual which lacks Christianity's doctrine of a special, loving relationship between God and the human individual.
13–14	*aptest in contrivance . . . stopping such* the medical skill of delaying the escape of the soul by healing the body and deferring its death.
17	*snakestone* a substance used in the treatment of snake-bites.
28	*Vespasian* Roman Emperor (AD 70–9) who invaded Palestine in 66; his son Titus sacked Jerusalem in 70.
30	*balls* eyeballs.
36	*Bethany* the home of Lazarus, a village near Jerusalem.
40	*travel-scrip* travelling bag or pouch.

42	*viscid choler . . . observable* glutinous bile; Karshish notes the predominant sickness of the area.
43	*tertians* fevers recurring every third day.
44	*falling-sickness* epilepsy.
49	*runagate* vagabond, renegade. Karshish does not wish to write out the cure for 'falling-sickness' that he has learned lest it be stolen by this 'runagate' carrier of his letter to Abib.
50–1	*His service . . . ailing eye* i.e. the carrier is delivering the letter in payment for Karshish's treatment of his bad eye.
55	*gum-tragacanth* a salve.
57	*porphyry* hard stone used as the mortar for pestle-grinding.
60	*Zoar* town near Dead Sea.
67	*tang* sting.
69	*The Man* Lazarus.
79	*subinduced* brought about as a symptom or result of something else.
81	*three days* in John 11:17,39 Lazarus was in the tomb for four days.
82	*exhibition* administration, application.
89	*conceit* fancy, imagining. Karshish refers to what he takes as Lazarus' delusion – on his sudden return from epileptic trance – that he has been raised from the dead.
103	*fume* hallucination.
106	*saffron* orange-yellow dye derived from the plant of the same name.
109	*Sanguine* red-blooded; strong.
	fifty years At the time Karshish is supposed to have met him, Lazarus would have been at least some ten years older. The facts of the Lazarus story as given by Karshish are sometimes at variance with the details of the Gospel version (see also l. 81n and l. 252n). The point may be to lend a verisimilitude to the representation of Karshish as the teller of a story which he does not know directly.
137	*The golden mean* 'the avoidance of excess and defect' (OED).
161	*pretermission* neglect, overlooking.

167   *lord*   teacher.

169   *mind*   remember.

167–73   *he regards thee . . . into stars*   i.e. when Karshish questions Lazarus' attention to apparently insignificant things ('Demand / The reason why', ll. 165–6), Lazarus regards Karshish in the same manner as the teacher of both Abib and Karshish had looked at his two pupils when they 'unadvisedly' (l. 170) recited a powerful charm from his 'book' (l. 171).

174–7   *Thou . . . did ye know!*   The words of the teacher of Abib and Karshish, warning them that they are like children in their ignorance of or blindness to ('veil', l. 174) what they are doing when they recite a powerful charm; they are 'playing with fire'. Karshish compares the way in which this teacher knew of things hidden from ordinary sight with Lazarus' way of viewing ordinary reality as if he knew of things higher than the world.

177   *Greek fire*   an incendiary mixture, actually invented later than the time of Karshish.

179   *It . . . perforcedly*   i.e. he leads his life only because he has to.

194   *tick*   beat of the pulse.

213   *affects*   aspires, desires.

228   *affects*   feel affection for.

240   *sublimed*   refined.

247   *leech*   physician.

248   *tumult*   Pilate delivered Christ to the people after 'a tumult was made' (Matthew 27:24).

252   *earthquake*   the earthquake occurring at Christ's death; see Matthew 27:51. Karshish's account of the events surrounding Christ's death are garbled.

281   *borage*   herb, once used medicinally as a stimulant.
             Aleppo   town in Syria.

'CHILDE ROLAND TO THE DARK TOWER CAME'

Date of composition uncertain (possibly early 1852); first published *1855*.

This account of a psychological journey or quest is partly informed by Browning's familiarity with medieval chivalric romance, fairy-tale and folk-lore, the Bible and other sources (including, of course, Shakespeare), none of which influences the poem as a uniquely authoritative model. In 1887 Browning noted: 'I was conscious of no allegorical intention in writing it. . . . Childe Roland came upon me as kind of dream. I had to write it. . . . it was simply that I had to do it. I did not know then what I meant beyond that, and I'm sure I don't know now. But I am very fond of it' (DeVane 1955: p. 229). Isobel Armstrong comments: 'It is a miasmic poem of continually dissolving certainties and contradictions. . . . what the knight does is to walk a psychological treadmill, repeating the same experience in a multitude of different and ever more violent ways. The imagery is all circular, even though it may look superficially as though some progress has been made. . . . these are the tortured images of a person who is trapped in his own fears and fantasies, the self-created prison of his own identity. The knight sees his quest in terms of an escape from the self, the search for some revelation from without. But he is forced to confront himself and to go deeper and deeper into the dark regions of his being. . . . The dark tower corresponds to the . . . "inmost centre" from which truth can be derived in *Paracelsus*, but . . . confidence in the creating mind has darkened. . . . high Romantic optimism is soberly qualified in this mature poem' (Armstrong 1969: pp. 300–2). Harold Bloom observes: 'Childe Roland . . . is painter as well as poet, and dies as a living picture, framed by "all the lost adventurers my peers" [l. 195], who like him found all things deformed and broken. All this is the living circumference of ' "Childe Roland to the Dark Tower Came" '; we move to the central meaning when we ponder the sorrow of this quester, this *aware* solipsist whose self-recognition has ceased to be an avenue to freedom' (Bloom 1971: pp. 165–6). See Introduction, pp. 1–2 and Critical Commentary, p. 180.

Title	These words are spoken by Edgar in *King Lear*, III. iv. 179. 'Childe' is the title of a young warrior striving to prove himself worthy of knighthood. Roland was a hero of the eleventh-century French romance *Chanson de Roland*; his story told in numerous versions, in different languages, throughout the Middle Ages and beyond. Edgar's line in *Lear* is a disconnected fragment uttered while he is feigning madness. The line, with its detail of the tower, is 'Probably . . . from a lost ballad' (Kenneth Muir (ed.) (1972) *King Lear*, Arden 9th edition, London, Methuen).
25–36	*As when . . . love and stay* These lines include an echo of John Donne's 'A Valediction: Forbidding Mourning', ll. 1–4.
48	*estray* stray creature; i.e. the speaker.
58	*cockle, spurge* weeds.
59	*none to awe* none to awe them into submission (check their growth); or, the landscape is so desolate it contains none that they might awe by their growth.
60	*burr* a clinging seed-pod.
64	*It nothing skills* It is no use.
66	*Calcine* burn to ashes or powder. The fallen forms of nature (or, emblematically, of the mind) cannot be purged ('set . . . free') until the final Day of Judgement.
68	*bents* coarse grasses.
70	*dock* coarse, broad-leaved, weedy plant, useful for treating nettle-stings.
	to baulk to check, refuse, deny.
72	*Pashing* dashing, trampling.
76	*stiff blind horse* suggested in part by the figure of a horse in a tapestry owned by Browning (Orr 1896: p. 274).
80	*colloped* the relevant sense of 'collop' here seems to be that of a 'slice of meat' (OED).
90	*One . . . to rights* Childe Roland decides to think of better times in the past to offset the unpleasantness of his present experience. Yet as he remembers old acquaintances in the next two stanzas (Cuthbert, l. 91; Giles, l. 97), he faces the fact that the old days were not

simply good, but characterized also by degradation and treachery.

99   *What . . . he durst* 'I dare do all that may become a man; / Who dares do more is none' (*Macbeth* I. vii. 46–7).

106   *howlet* owl, owlet.

114   *bespate* bespattered, spat on.
       spumes foamings.

116   *alders* shrubby trees.

128   *presage* prediction of the future.

131   *plash* mire.

133   *fell cirque* terrible (circular) space, dreadful natural arena.

135   *mews* here 'mew': cage, coop, place of confinement.

136   *Mad* maddening.

137–8 *galley-slaves . . . pastime* the Turk sets galley-slaves against each other for entertainment.

141   *brake* a 'heavy harrow for crushing clods'; a 'toothed instrument for braking flax or hemp' (OED).

143   *Tophet* Israelite valley of burning; symbolic of Hell.

145   *stubbed* abounding in stubs, stumps.

149   *rood* quarter of an acre.

160   *Apollyon* in Revelation 9:11 'the angel of the bottom-less pit'; in the first part of Bunyan's *Pilgrim's Progress* Apollyon has 'wings like a dragon'.

161   *dragon-penned* with flight-feathers like a dragon.

167   *solve it, you!* Childe Roland's self-address?; or, a pro-to–postmodernist invitation to the reader to make sense of the sudden transitions and transformations in which the poem deals?

179   *nonce* crucial moment.

181–2 *the Tower . . . turret* Browning commented in 1866 that the literal appearance of the Tower was suggested by 'some recollection of a strange solitary little tower I have come upon more than once in Massa-Carrara, in the midst of low hills' (DeVane and Knickerbocker 1950: p. 173).

185   *unseen shelf* hidden sandbank or rocks (whose exist-ence is realized only when the ship founders).

192   *heft* hilt.

203   *slug-horn* properly 'slughorn', an early form of 'slogan' (battle-cry). Thomas Chatterton used the word erroneously to mean a trumpet (OED) and Browning here uses it in the same way to mean some kind of (battle) horn. In the legends, Roland, outnumbered by the Saracens at Roncevaux, refused to blow his horn to summon help from the Emperor Charlemagne until it was too late. Having sounded his horn, Roland, sole survivor of his company, died just after hearing Charlemagne's forces coming to the rescue.

LOVE IN A LIFE

Date of composition unknown; first published *1855*.

Critics have seen in this, as in its companion piece 'Life in a Love', Browning's expression of his own happiness with Elizabeth Barrett as contrasted with the unhappiness of some lovers. There are perhaps certain imagistic parallels with a letter of 5 April 1846 from Browning to Elizabeth Barrett: 'In this House of Life – where I go, you go, – where I ascend you run before, – where I descend, it is after you' (Kintner 1969: II, p. 591). For another kind of reading, see Critical Commentary, pp. 159–61.

7   *cornice-wreath* one sense of 'cornice' is an 'ornamental moulding running round the wall of a room, etc' (OED); here the ornament would presumably be some kind of floral-wreath.

LIFE IN A LOVE

First published *1855*. See notes to 'Love in a Life'.

THE LAST RIDE TOGETHER

Date of composition unknown; first published *1855*.

The poem 'depicts the emotions of a ride, which a finally dismissed lover has been allowed to take with his beloved' (Orr 1896: p. 295). Long appreciated as a literal love poem, the work has also been read as self-referential; that is, as concerned with the relations between the speaker and his Muse (see I. Orenstein, *Baylor Browning Interests*, 18, 1964: pp. 3–10). Compare 'Love in a Life' and 'Life in a Love'.

62   *Ten lines*   the lines of an obituary-notice.
65   *They . . . Abbey-stones*   he is honoured with burial and a memorial in Westminster Abbey.
88   *in fine*   in short.
90   *sublimate*   refine, elevate.

ANDREA DEL SARTO

Probably written 1852–3; first published *1855*.

The Florentine painter Andrea (1486–1530) was called 'del Sarto' because his father was a tailor and 'the Faultless Painter' because of the excellence of his technique. He married a widow, Lucrezia del Fede, in about 1518 and shortly thereafter (1518–19) he was in the French court of Francis I. One of Browning's 'sources' is a painting which in his day hung in the Pitti Palace, Florence, and was ascribed to Andrea (the attribution has since been questioned). The work, supposedly of the painter and his wife, shows a man of sad expression holding his arm around the shoulders of a woman with whom he is apparently pleading but who looks coldly away. Setting his poem in 1525, Browning 'imagines Andrea on the evening when he conceived' the Pitti portrait (DeVane 1955: p. 245). *Vasari*, Browning's principal source, describes Lucrezia as overbearing and mercenary, exercising a deleterious influence over Andrea that cost him the respect of his associates. Informing Browning's representation of Andrea is Vasari's opinion that the painter's work was technically faultless but that his timidity of nature prevented him from instilling passion into his art. Some modern scholarship has seen Vasari's view of Andrea – exaggerated further in Browning's characterization, which can be viewed as a study in moral inadequacy or cowardice – as unfairly biased.

15   *Fiesole*   a hill-town north east of Florence.
29   *everybody's moon*   Andrea used his wife's face in his

paintings of women ('It saves a model', l. 25) and his wife in that sense becomes public property; but there may also be an insinuation that she is faithless.

35   *common greyness*   thought in Browning's day to be a feature of Andrea's work (and isolated by Browning as a symptom of his character); but modern scholarship has tended to attribute the quality to processes of ageing and fading.

42–3   *That length . . . inside*   The image of contained security is typical of Andrea in Browning's characterization; see also ll. 169–70.

57   *cartoon*   preparatory sketch for a painting.

65   *Legate*   Pope's envoy.

76   *Someone*   Michelangelo; see l. 130n.

93   *Morello*   a mountain near Florence.

105   *The Urbinate . . . ago*   Raphael (1483–1520) was born at Urbino; the reference dates the poem's setting as 1525.

106   *Vasari*   Giorgio Vasari (1511–74), author of *Lives of the Artists*.

130   *Agnolo*   Michelangelo (1475–1564).

146   *fear . . . Paris lords*   Andrea left his well-paid work during 1518–19 at the French court of Francis I because a letter from Lucrezia urged him to return to Florence. Tradition had it that he left promising to return with works of art, for which Francis I had provided money, but that he used the funds for his own ends, never returning to France and incurring the French King's anger. Thus his embarrassment at meeting French lords. Andrea, here as elsewhere, tends self-pityingly to blame his wife for having damaged his chances of becoming a great painter; a painter, for example, like Raphael (l. 152). Modern scholars have challenged the accuracy of the story of Andrea's abduction of the money.

150   *Fontainebleau*   town south–east of Paris, site of Francis I's royal palace.

155   *mouth's . . . smile*   the smiling mouth that indicated approval of my work.

178   *Roman*   Raphael, who worked in Rome.

210	*cue-owls* Scops-owls, named in Italy after the sound of their cry ('chiu', pronounced *cue*).
220	*Cousin* a Renaissance euphemism for 'lover'; the implication is more nearly that of prostitution in l. 222.
241	*scudi* Roman coins.
261–2	*Four . . . angel's reed* see Revelation 21: 10–21.
263	*Leonard* Leonardo da Vinci (1452–1519).
265–6	*still . . . choose* Again, Andrea thinks of his marriage as accounting for his artistic inferiority in comparison with the unmarried da Vinci, Raphael and Michelangelo (l. 263). But he does not simply blame his wife. He allows, at last, that it is his choice – albeit one which he holds uneasily – not to put his work above all else.

CLEON

Probably written 1854; first published *1855*.

The poem presents Cleon as a pagan philosopher-poet writing a letter in response to inquiries sent him from a patron-king, Protus. The poem is set during the early years of Christianity (about AD 52); both Cleon and Protus are fictional. Cleon's pagan philosophy means that while he 'believes in Zeus under the attributes of the one God' (Orr 1896: p. 193), he has no belief in personal immortality and is dismissive of what he has heard of Christian doctrine (ll. 337–53). 'Cleon' was possibly suggested by Matthew Arnold's 'Empedocles on Etna' (1852), which shows Empedocles as a pagan Greek philosopher who takes his own life through despair at the human condition. Browning is understood by some commentators to be highlighting the inadequacies of a thought-system which does not offer ideas of a loving God, or of potential human redemption and personal immortality. He is also sometimes thought to be hinting, in certain aspects of his representation of Cleon, that there is, latently, a universal human need for spiritual reassurances akin to those offered by Christianity. The poem relates to Victorian debates about the relative claims of sceptical intellectual inquiry and religious faith. See Critical Commentary, p. 166.

Epigraph   from Acts 17:28, where St Paul, preaching at Athens, makes a connection between the Christian idea of

God and sentiments expressed by classical pagan poets: 'For in him [God] we live, and move, and have our being; as certain also of your own poets have said'.

1   *sprinkled isles*   probably the Sporades, scattered Greek islands in the Aegean.

4   *Tyranny*   used in its Greek sense as a description of absolute rule, without necessarily implying appalling oppression.

10   *Royal . . . sunset*   purple and crimson were royal colours.

14   *settle-down*   flock settling (settled) down.

15   *lyric*   beautiful.
        crocus   saffron.

16   *sea-wools*   wools dyed with sea–purple (derived from a kind of shellfish yielding purple dye).

26   *tower*   a monument commissioned by Protus; the account of the building suggests an allegory of human aspiration towards the heavens.

43   *requirement*   inquiry, question, request.

47   *epos*   epic, heroic poem.

48   *little chant*   song.

51   *phare*   lighthouse.

53   *Poecile*   the painted Portico or colonnade at Athens.

60   *moods*   modes: types of musical scale in ancient Greek music.

64–71   *We of these . . . for ours*   Comparing the knowledge of his own day with that of an earlier period (the 'heroic age', l. 70), Cleon observes that greater and more complex understanding may be associated with dissociation and fragmentation ('the small part of a man of us', l. 69), as contrasted with the integrity of mind belonging to a simpler age ('some whole man', l. 70). The point is connected with Victorian anxieties that increasing knowledge in all realms of human inquiry was threatening traditional bases of psychological and cultural health. Compare 'Love Among the Ruins'.

83   *rhomb*   equilateral parallelogram.

84   *lozenge*   diamond–shaped figure.

	trapezoid four-sided figure without parallel sides.
97	*rounds* defines the limits of.
99–113	*It takes . . . our life* i.e., the simpler minds of the ancients could reach, like water in a partially-filled sphere, the furthest limits of human knowledge only at one point at a time; while the more sophisticated mind of Cleon's day can, like air in a sphere, touch an entire range of points at the same time. Like air, however, the sophisticated mind's powers are not visible and hence are 'misknown' (l. 112). Despite Cleon's defence of the 'modern' mind, he will acknowledge that such a mind does not necessarily have peace of mind.
132	*The suave . . . drupe* the sweet as against the bitter wild plum.
138	*soul* 'Cleon constantly uses the word soul as antithesis to body: but he uses it in its ancient . . . sense, as expressing the sentient life, not the spiritual' (Orr 1896: p. 194).
140	*Terpander* seventh-century BC musician of Lesbos, supposed to have invented the seven-string lyre.
141	*Phidias . . . friend* Phidias was a fifth-century BC Greek sculptor and painter; the friend is apparently the Athenian statesman Pericles (c. 500–429 BC).
148–9	*pricked . . . wine* tempered sweetness with the sharper flavour of wine; i.e., mixed different kinds of thought and achievement.
212	*intro-active* internally active.
224	*sense of sense* self-consciousness, reason.
246	*recipiency* receptivity.
249	*It skills not* it is no use.
252	*Naiad* water-nymph.
258	*boots* use.
268–9	*where is . . . answer* an instance of Cleon's frustration at being unable to find grounds for faith in a loving God.
273–335	*The last . . . possible* the idea, the validity of which Cleon refuses, that there is a sufficient kind of immortality in the works a person leaves behind, was one held by Victorian adherents of Utilitarianism and Positivism.

288   *Phoebus*   Apollo, god of the sun and poetry.

304   *Sappho*   seventh-century BC lyric poetess from the Greek island of Lesbos.

305   *Æschylus*   the Athenian tragic poet (525–456 BC).

332   *fly*   butterfly (a symbol of the spiritual soul).

333   *wants*   meaning both 'lacks' and 'desires'.

340   *Paulus*   St Paul.

341   *Indeed . . . with him*   Cleon speculates that St Paul and Christ may be the same person (the point emphasizes Cleon's ignorance; but Browning at the same time glances surreptitiously at the sense in which so much Christian doctrine finds its early formulation in the writings of St Paul).

TWO IN THE CAMPAGNA

Probably written May 1854; first published *1855*.

In May 1854 the Brownings were in Rome and spent, according to Elizabeth Barrett, 'some exquisite hours on the Campagna' (the country plain around Rome and the site of ancient Latian cities; Kenyon 1897: II, p. 165). The poem has been read as both autobiographical and as a dramatic monologue. See Critical Commentary, pp. 152–8.

15   *weft*   web.

21   *champaign*   campagna.

33   *As earth . . . above!*   The line perhaps contains an allusion to the myth in which Zeus ravished Danaë, descending on her in a shower of gold ('Now lies the Earth all Danaë to the stars', Tennyson, *The Princess*, VII. 168). The allusion would be relevant to the speaker's debate in these stanzas about the problematical relationship between natural impulse and psychological / moral restraint.

48   *pluck the rose*   'When I have plucked the rose, / I cannot give it vital growth again; / It needs must wither' (*Othello*, V.ii.13–15).

55   *Fixed*   oriented and placed (through having a 'fix' on a star: a navigational metaphor).

The larger part probably written 1862 in Brittany: Browning stayed in a house in Sainte Marie, a seaside hamlet near Pornic, in the summers of 1862 and 1863 (the view from the house providing the details of fig-tree and field in section III). First published *1864*; incorporating, as stanzas 1–6 of section VI, verse which Browning had published under the title 'Lines' in the *Monthly Repository* for May 1836.

The work is a kind of interior monologue, 'spoken' by James Lee's wife. It traces her reflections and feelings as she slowly and painfully comes to terms with an awareness that her husband's love for her has faded. The poem 'is a lyrical monodrama, the moods taking the places of characters' (DeVane 1955: p. 286). Different moods or phases of reflection are associated with different physical locations or activities in each section; thus *V On the Cliff* or *VI Reading a Book, Under the Cliff*, etc. In both overall structural procedure (radically disjunct for the time) and detailed poetic manner the poem (particularly in section V) recalls aspects of Tennyson's *Maud. A Monodrama* (1855). The preoccupations of George Meredith's *Modern Love* (published April 1862) may also have had a general influence. Browning commented on the couple represented in the poem: 'I meant them for . . . people newly-married, trying to realize a dream of being sufficient to each other, in a foreign land (where you can try such an experiment) and finding it break up – the man being tired *first*, – and tired precisely of the love' (Curle 1937: p. 123). See Critical Commentary, p. 158.

72	*bent*	coarse grass stalk.
76–9	*To the spirit . . . cold*	i.e., to the spirit (that) God meant . . . . An idealistic view of the spiritual power of the married state. James Lee's wife has slowly to work herself out of attachment to such a view.
105–6	*rivers . . . Book assures*	No single passage in the Bible is apparently referred to; but for oil and wine as tokens of richness and happiness, see Joel 2:24 and Deuteronomy 8:7–10.
137	*barded*	bard: 'A covering of armour for the breast and flanks of a war-horse' (OED).

	chanfroned chamfron: 'The frontlet of a barded horse' (OED).
138	*quixote-mage* magician or seer with the qualities of Don Quixote ('visionary . . . inspired by . . . unrealizable ideals', OED).
143	*fans* wings.
VI	*Reading a Book, Under the Cliff* As noted above, the first six stanzas of this section are an incorporation of early lines by Browning himself. Here they are presented as quotations from the 'Book' read by James Lee's wife, so that there is an element of self-referential irony on Browning's part when he has the wife observe in l. 182 that the verse lines come 'from some young man's pride'.
227	*grave* engrave.
244–69	*As like . . . fingertips* James Lee's wife is drawing the hand of a 'little girl' (see ll. 292–3). She sees evidence of divine creativity and love in the beauty of the living hand and she contemplates the impossibility of matching that beauty in her drawing. As she draws she fantasizes (ll. 262–9) a means of injecting transcendent spiritual passion (see l. 268: 'grace') into a human work of art.
257	*limit-line* outline: here, specifically, the utmost limit of the human capacity to represent beauty, which still falls short of ideal beauty.
270–91	*'Tis a . . . bride* James Lee's wife now thinks of a clay cast of a hand made by Leonardo da Vinci (1452–1519) and of how even such a 'master' (l. 274) artist met his 'match' (l. 275) and 'could not emulate / The beauty' (ll. 277–8) in the cast taken from life. So the 'god' (l. 280) da Vinci, like James Lee's wife the 'worm' (in matters of art, l. 281), had to learn that the spiritual ideal will always exceed the possibilities of human representation (see ll. 290–1).
292–332	*Little girl . . . understand* A passage which shows James Lee's wife recognizing positively that the individual cannot achieve absolute fulfilment in life. Imagining da Vinci speaking to her she develops a view – based on the model of artistic attempts to represent perfect beauty –

that experience is a matter of the activity of striving towards completeness rather than of idealistically imagining that completeness is actually available in mortal life. The 'use' of life is one of process rather than of the achievement of a total, consummatory end. Recognition at a profound imaginative level that life does not stop when love is unreciprocated provides James Lee's wife with the psychological strength to accept, in section IX of the poem, that she cannot hold on to one whose love for her is exhausted.

313   *outer sheath*   skin.

325   *strait dole*   restricted, impoverished allowance.

368–71   *Why, fade . . . myself.*   James Lee's wife's acceptance that she must 'set' her husband 'free' (l. 337) is no trite or complacent formula; as is shown in her continuing expression of love for him throughout this section and in the disturbing image of her in these closing lines, where, unlike her husband, she is tired not *of* love but exhausted and withered by her own capacities *for* love. Compare 'Two in the Campagna'.

ABT VOGLER

Date of composition unknown; first published *1864*.

Abt (Abbot) Georg Joseph Vogler (1749–1814) was a German musician, of considerable note in his day, who had been the master of John Relfe, Browning's own childhood music-teacher. Vogler invented the orchestrion, a species of organ. He was known as a great extemporizer and in Browning's poem is depicted just after he has been playing a brilliant extempore exercise 'upon the musical instrument of his invention'. He meditates sorrowfully on the passing of an inspired moment of artistic performance, finding consolation in the belief that that moment of apparently unearthly achievement, though never to be regained in this life, is a type of what is eternally present in heaven (see l. 72).

1   *structure*   the word lays the foundation of the analogy between architectural form and the pattern of musical

performance that Vogler will develop, in ll. 3–8, in his allusion to legends concerning the Old Testament King Solomon.

brave splendid.

3–8 *as when . . . palace* In the Old Testament, God's name (represented by the letters JHVH; later supplemented to produce the artificial form Jehovah) was thought of as a profound mystery, not susceptible of utterance. But in Talmudic tradition (i.e. a body of writings including commentary on the Old Testament), Solomon was supposed to have received from heaven a ring which bore on it the name of God and which, giving Solomon the power to speak 'the ineffable Name' (l. 7), gave him the power to command supernatural agencies, both angelic and demonic. Solomon was supposed to have called on these forces to assist him in the construction of the buildings at Jerusalem; including, in Browning's poem, a palace for 'the princess' (l. 8), Pharoah's daughter (see 1 Kings 7:8). The allusion to arcane energies registers Vogler's sense of the more than earthly dimension of his own inspired musical performance.

11 *dispart* separate.

12 *heighten . . . praise* increase their master's admiration. The distance Vogler sets up between himself (the 'master') and the keys of the instrument he is playing is a way of conveying his sense of having been inspired; of having been possessed by a power not simply his own.

16 *nether springs* the deepest, darkest foundation or source of things. The connection between this foundation and possibly hellish fire ('fearless of flame') continues the association, established in the earlier reference to Solomon's 'angels' and 'demons' (l. 4), between inspiration and superhuman energies that have simultaneously light and dark valencies.

19 *rampired* ramparted.

21–3 *runner . . . spire* the dome of St Peter's, Rome, used on certain festivals to be illuminated by 'runners' with burning lamps.

25–32 *In sight . . . nor far* Vogler is describing how, in his moment of inspiration, his soul had seemed to communicate directly with heaven; the gap between 'Nature' (l. 26) and the divine having apparently been closed.

33   *there wanted not who*   there was no lack of those who.

34   *fresh from the Protoplast*   newly created; the Protoplast is 'the original, archetype'; the 'first former, fashioner, or creator' (OED). The fire of Vogler's inspiration embraces spiritual forms that do not reside in the ordinary world.

35   *Furnished*   endowed.

41–56   *All through . . . the head.*   The idea running through these stanzas is that the visual and verbal arts, however finely constructed, are still subject to mundane laws and are lower kinds of art than music, whose essence and inspiration derives more directly from God.

66   *houses . . . hands*   2 Corinthians 5:1: 'a building of God, an house not made with hands.'

70–2   *The evil . . . round*   Vogler is stating a belief that no good is lost (however it may appear on earth), but a greater good grows out of the encounter with evil. On earth there are only glimpses (the 'broken arcs' of Vogler's performative inspiration) of the ultimately total good ('in the heaven, a perfect round').

82   *fulness of the days*   'That in the dispensation of the fulness of times he might gather together in one all things in Christ, both which are in heaven, and which are on earth' (Ephesians 1:10).

84   *discords . . . prized*   the loss of the perfect moment enables harmony – the idea of the heavenly perfect round – to be appreciated more.

89–96   *Well . . . to sleep*   As Vogler subsides from the moment of his inspired rapture he describes his return to day-to-day reality in musical terms. He pictures himself feeling again for the 'common chord' (l. 91) and 'Sliding by semitones' (l. 92) to the 'C-major' (l. 96) of normal life (the chord has no sharps or flats).

93   *alien ground*   the normal plane of life is alien from the heavenly raptures he has just left.

Probably not composed before 1859 (see below): first published *1864*.

The speaker of this monologue is an incurable religious optimist. Abraham Ibn Ezra, or Abenezra, was a twelfth-century Spanish Jewish scholar, who spent the later part of his life travelling in exile to escape persecution in Spain. In writing the poem Browning seems partly to have had in mind Edward FitzGerald's translation of *The Rubáiyát of Omar Khayyám* (1859). Browning's Ben Ezra articulates a vision directly contrasting with the metaphysical pessimism and despairing hedonism of FitzGerald's speaker. See Critical Commentary, pp. 165–6.

7–15	*Not that . . . remonstrate* Ben Ezra's awkward inversion amounts to a statement that, in his high estimation of old age, he is not remonstrating against the tendency of youth to overvalue particular selections from experience ('"Which rose . . ."', l. 8) while at the same time desiring a totality beyond the particularities of experience ('". . . transcends them all!"', l.12).
12	*figured flame* imagined star.
24	*Irks . . . beast?* do care and doubt bother well-fed animals? For Ben Ezra it is the 'Irks' and 'Frets' which define the spiritual 'spark' (l.18) of humanity and without which human beings are indistinguishable from animal creation ('Low kinds', l. 17).
25–7	*Rejoice . . . not receive* Rejoice that human kind is allied to the divine principle ('That', l. 26) which is active in giving. The non-human creation simply takes what is provided by God (hence it is the distinction of human kind that it can 'effect' and 'not receive!', l. 27).
29	*hold of* are related to.
30	*tribes that take* the non-human creatures that simply take.
39	*Shall . . . fail* an inversion: life shall succeed in that it seems to fail.
42	*scale* the scale of the chain of being.
45	*want* lack.

49	*gifts* human endowments.
55	*Not once beat* i.e., should the heart not once beat . . . ?
62	*rose-mesh* the net of the flesh, with its blood-vessels.
64–6	*Would we . . . best* Ben Ezra acknowledges that it would, in fact, be nice if humanity could find some spiritual fulfilment to match the way in which mere animals can satisfy physical desire.
71–2	*Let us . . . soul!* Ben Ezra again refuses a complete denigration of the physical side of human nature. It is through a balancing of the physical and spiritual sides of that nature that Ben Ezra seeks a model for human satisfaction.
84	*indue* put on.
85	*try* test, endeavour to find out. In this and the following stanza Ben Ezra finds images to suggest that in old age it will be possible to look back over past years and to distil a wisdom that will be of value in facing what is still to come.
102	*proved* tested.
107–8	*The master . . . play* These lines anticipate the metaphor of the potter's wheel in ll. 150ff.
113	*tempt* attempt.
139–40	*all . . . plumb* everything in a previous life that cannot be quantified.
141	*passed* passed over, ignored.
150	*God . . . shaped* the metaphor of the individual as a pot made (turned on the wheel) by God occurs in the *Rubáiyát*. (See also Isaiah 64:8). The image of the spiritual pot gathers for Ben Ezra all those qualities of individual life which, in the preceding stanzas, he has said are ignored by the 'low world' (l. 137) and its material considerations. In Ben Ezra's formulations (ll. 153, 162) the potter's wheel turns in time, but the pot, the individual, is spiritual and the shaping hands divine. Some commentators have suggested that the image bears a worrying connotation that the human spirit does not have free will.
154–6	*Thou . . . today!* Ben Ezra addresses someone who holds the (drunken) opinion that since life is short then the pleasures of the moment should be indulged in.

Such was the opinion (and inebriation the recommendation) of the speaker in the *Rubáiyát*.

165–8   *This . . . impressed*   i.e., this Present you would hold on to is a mechanism designed to examine and test your soul, etc.

168   *Try*   test.

169–74   *What . . . sterner stress?*   These lines present youth and age in terms of a pot being shaped. The 'base' (l. 171) is youth; while 'Scull-things' (l. 173) is age or approaching death and proximity to God ('Master's lips', l. 179).

174   *sterner stress*   heavier pressure.

178   *new wine*   spiritual essence.

CALIBAN UPON SETEBOS

Date of composition unknown, but possibly after 1859 (see below); first published *1864*.

The poem develops Shakespeare's Caliban, the man-beast of *The Tempest*, as its speaker. Browning's 'Caliban is much exercised by the government of the world, and by the probable nature of its ruler; and he has filched an hour from his tasks, on a summer noon, when Prospero and Miranda are taking his diligence upon trust, to go and sprawl full length in the mud of some cave, and talk the problem out' (Orr 1896: p. 195). Browning may have been stimulated by Darwin's *Origin of Species* (November 1859) to imagine an early evolutionary stage in human explanation of the world. On the relation of the poem to nineteenth-century Higher Criticism and natural theology, see Critical Commentary, pp. 167–8 and pp. 180–1.

Epigraph   a misquotation (deliberately ironic?) from Psalm 50:21, where God speaks to the Godless: 'thou thoughtest wickedly, that I am even such a one as thyself.'

1   *['Will sprawl*   *I* will sprawl. Pronouns (often the lack of them) are a special feature of the poem. What Caliban calls the 'Quiet' is referred to in the neuter as 'it' (e.g. l. 137), while 'Setebos' is designated as 'He', always *with*

the capital (e.g. ll. 24–5). Caliban refers to himself very occasionally in the first person but mainly he speaks of himself in the third person ('he', as in l. 4; or 'his', as in l. 2, *without* capitals); and sometimes, as in this opening line, he uses no pronoun at all (when the omission is represented by an apostrophe). Caliban's use of the third person in self-reference, or his omission of person altogether, suggests an uncertainty about his own identity that is part and parcel of his uncertainty about the nature of the world and its government. The brackets around the first twenty-three lines (as around the concluding twelve) indicate that Caliban is thinking to himself rather than talking out loud.

5   *eft-things*   newts and the like.

7   *pompion*   pumpkin.

16   *dam*   mother. In *The Tempest* Caliban's mother is Sycorax and her God is Setebos.

17   *Him, vexes*   Setebos is vexed when he is talked about.

20   *Prosper*   Prospero, the master of Caliban in *The Tempest*.
Miranda   Prospero's daughter in *The Tempest*.

23   *rank*   includes an old meaning – 'rebellious'.

27   *not the stars*   In Caliban's speculations later in the poem (ll. 137–8) he suggest that the stars are the realm of 'Quiet', which he posits as a greater principle than the god Setebos. Caliban's metaphysics are not dogmatically certain but expressly exploratory, so that he shifts his definitions from time to time. But Setebos and Quiet emerge as the two main propositions.

43   *He*   Setebos, in Caliban's thought, is a divine power, a kind of *demiurge* – maker of the world but not, like Quiet, the ultimate principle of the universe – who is locked into a relationship with the world that is characterized by self-loathing, by desire and envy, attraction and repulsion (see ll. 56–62). Caliban thus accounts for the imperfect, distorted and contradictory character of creation. Demiurge: 'A name for the Maker of the world, in the Platonic philosophy; in the Gnostic system, conceived as a being subordinate to the Supreme Being, and sometimes as the author of evil' (OED).

44	*thereat* thereupon, because of that ('Hating and loving warmth', l. 43).
47	*auk* a type of sea-bird.
50	*pie* possibly magpie or pied woodpecker.
51	*oakwarts* probably oak galls.
66–7	*Because . . . plague* Even though the things of the world made by Setebos may be braver and better than their progenitor, they are powerless ('nothing skills') if Setebos imposes suffering on them ('begin to plague').
68	*I* Caliban's first use of the first person, significantly at the moment in the poem when he begins to exercise direct power over other created things. There is a suggested correlation – negative in many of its connotations – between power and identity.
71	*bladdery* bubbly.
72	*maggots* the beverage Caliban has made produces a disturbance in his mind.
74	*wanton* Caliban too is infected by frustration and desire.
75	*Put case* suppose that.
79	*hoopoe* colourful crested bird.
83	*grigs* grasshoppers or crickets.
103	*Loving . . . so* merely an arbitrary faculty of choice, motivated by neither love nor hate; like the amorality defined in l. 98.
127–31	*But wherefore . . . perchance* Caliban thinks that only the principle that made and is greater than Setebos might be asked to explain Setebos' nature. But, Caliban reflects momentarily, perhaps Setebos has already destroyed his own maker.
132–42	*There . . . many-handed* Developing the idea that there is still 'something over' (l. 129) Setebos, Caliban speculates that Quiet, as ultimate principle, has no lack, no desire, no vulnerable capacity for joy or suffering, and hence is completely indifferent to the travails of created things. This Quiet may constitute a peace unto itself but that very self-sufficiency means that, in practical terms, it is irrelevant to Caliban, who must concern himself with the proximately active power, Setebos.
143–7	*Who . . . real* The motivating force out of which

Caliban's world was created was Setebos' spite at not having peace himself.

148	*hips* fruits of the wild rose.
156	*oncelot* ocelot or jaguar.
157	*ounce* lynx, cheetah, or snow-leopard.
161	*Ariel* Prospero's ethereal servant in *The Tempest*.
168–9	*'Plays . . . He* Setebos' created world has no more ultimately real substance than Prospero's or Caliban's own make-believes, fictions, fantasies.
171	*'holds not so* Caliban's mother's view that the Quiet made all things and that Setebos simply disturbs them is not true, for reasons Caliban expands upon in the following lines.
172	*meant* intended to produce.
177	*orc* a sea-creature, leviathan.
178	*He is the One now* again, Caliban stresses that the only divinity relevant to his experience is Setebos.
205	*wattles* twigs.
211	*ball* meteor, fire-ball.
214–15	*'Dug . . . a stone* a reference to a fossil.
216	*Please . . . does?* i.e., how do I please Setebos and prevent a fate befalling me such as that which befell the newt turned to stone – do I have to do as Prospero does?
229	*urchin* hedgehog.
250	*'Believeth . . . stop* Caliban believes that when life ends so, too, does pain.
251–2	*His dam . . . friends* Caliban rejects his mother's crude belief in a system of rewards and penalties after death.
258	*films* wings.
260	*painful . . . roll* beetles taking pains rolling.
288	*pillared . . . move* dust picked up in a whirlwind.

A LIKENESS

Probably written 1858 or 1859; first published *1864*.

The speaker of this poem draws three scenes, each presided over by a picture of a woman and each touching on questions of male feeling towards women. The first section (ll. 1–10) offers a scene of marriage, where the portrait of a woman is the focus of an implied jealousy on the wife's part and of implied frustration on the husband's part. The scene of the second section (ll. 11–32) is one of bachelordom and the symptoms of a distinct 'masculinity' ('foils . . . pipe-sticks . . . pistol-balls . . . cigar-case'). The portrait of a woman may have a certain pride of place but its role in this context is a disturbing one, since the suggestions of male exploitation and aggression carry throughout connotations of specifically sexual violence against women ('queen of the place . . . other spoils . . . the long whip . . . tandem-lasher . . . the Tipton Slasher . . . satin shoe used for cigar-case . . . the bruiser . . . the little edition of Rabelais . . . the eyes are half out of their sockets'). In the third section (ll. 33–69) the speaker tells us about a picture of a woman that is of great importance to him. The scene and significance of the picture are differentiated from the image of frustrated domesticity in the first section and from the rapacious male sexism of the second. Nor is the picture an instance simply of male spiritual idealization of woman. It fires a physical and a wider imaginative desire in the speaker ('cheeks grow red . . . heart leaps. . . . A face to lose youth for, to occupy age / With the dream of, meet death with'). But there remains frustration and rage issuing from a desire that can find no adequate expression or outlet ('a certain face, I never / Saw elsewhere touch or trace of / In women I've seen the face of').

6	*daub*	inferior painting.
10	*John's corns ail*	physical symptoms of the husband's sense of claustrophobia.
14	*masks, gloves and foils*	equipment used in fencing.
16	*tandem-lasher*	A tandem is a light two-wheeled carriage pulled by two horses one in front of the other (necessitating a long whip).
18	*the Tipton Slasher*	William Perry, from Tipton in Staffordshire. He became English boxing champion in 1850, losing the title in 1857 to Tom Sayers (see l. 23).
19	*the cards . . . ace*	Cards given a single mark (an 'ace') by a bullet.
20	*And . . . case*	An image of phallic penetration of the female.
21	*chamois*	a type of antelope.
	Chablais	a region in the French Alps.
22	*Rarey . . . Cruiser*	Browning bought J. S. Rarey's *Art*

	of Taming Horses in 1858. The book shows Rarey whipping his horse, 'Cruiser'.
23	*Sayers* see note to l. 18.
24	*Rabelais* French humourist and satirist (c.1494–c.1553); his writings were associated with sexual obscenity.
30	*proboscis* usually used of an elephant's trunk.
31	*Vichy* resort town in central France.
34	*mezzotint* an engraved print.
42	*imbroglio* a confused pile.
49	*pencil and lyre* art and music.
50	*National Portrait Gallery* in London.
54	*Marc Antonios* Marcantonio Raimondi, celebrated early-sixteenth-century Italian engraver.
55	*Festina Lentè!* go more slowly! Literally 'Make haste slowly' (Latin).
61	*Volpato's* Giovanni Volpato (1733–1803), well-known Italian engraver.

EPILOGUE

Probably written late 1863 or early 1864; first published *1864*. The names of the first and second speakers were introduced in the second edition of *Dramatis Personae*.

See Critical Commentary, pp. 168–9.

David	The Old Testament King David planned the temple at Jerusalem but it was built by Solomon after his death. Here, however, David not only thinks back on the building as completed but slips momentarily in his description from past to present tense (l. 11). The slippages of temporal perspective may be intended to suggest the way in which religious ritual conspires to repeat endlessly an originating formula, to reinscribe a founding (or founder's) truth.
1–2	the dedication of the Temple when the presence of the Lord was supposed to have entered it (see ll. 16–21; the occasion is described in 1 Kings 8, 9 and 2 Chronicles 5, 6).

3	*Levites* members of the tribe of Levi who assisted the priests in ritualistic observation.
Renan	The French scholar and philosopher Ernest Renan (1823–92), who historicized the life and denied the divinity of Christ in his *La Vie de Jésus* (1863). He did not arrive at his conclusions with ease of mind (see ll. 62–5).
24–5	*star . . . stood* includes an allusion to the star that 'stood' over Christ in the manger at Bethlehem (Matthew 2:9); an element of religious belief demythologized in Renan's thinking.
26	*Face* divine grace expressed in human form through Christ.
29	*gyre on gyre* spiral on spiral.
57	*disk's serene* the star of ll. 24–5, 31–40 and 60–1.
59–61	*Nor . . . fallen dumb?* In Renan's thought, a loving God does not exist outside of human projections.
62–5	*dread . . . falls!* With the old idea of God destroyed, humanity will curse at having to assume the prerogatives once ascribed to God.
66–101	*Witless . . . knows* For the general thought of these lines, see Critical Commentary, pp. 168–9. Mrs Orr registered the internalization of the divine in this section when, glossing Browning's use of the rock in Arctic seas (ll. 72–86) as an image of the individual human in all the vicissitudes of life (see ll. 87–92), she observed: 'in the Arctic Seas . . . the whole field of waters seem constantly hastening towards some central point of rock, to envelope it in their playfulness and force; in the blackness they have borrowed from the nether world, or the radiance they have caught from heaven; then tearing it up by the roots, to sweep onwards towards another peak, and make *it* their centre for the time being. So do the forces of life and nature circle round the individual . . . doing in each the work of experience, reproducing for each the Divine Face which is inspired by the spirit of creation. And, as the speaker declares, he needs no "Temple", because the world is that. Nor, as he implies, need he look beyond the range of his own being for . . . Divinity' (Orr 1896: p. 241).

82   *for a minute*   an allusion to the transitoriness of mortal life.
93   *one world*   the monism defined here (see Critical Commentary, pp. 168–9) has been anticipated in the picture of interfused heavenly and hellish colours in the description of the Arctic waves (ll. 78–80).
99   *one Face*   Browning commented: '"That Face," . . . "is the face of Christ. That is how I feel him"' (reported by Mrs Orr, *Contemporary Review*, 60, 1891: p. 880).

ESSAY ON SHELLEY

Late in 1851 Browning wrote an 'Introductory Essay' to the *Letters of Percy Bysshe Shelley*, a volume published early in 1852 by Edward Moxon. The book was withdrawn when it was discovered that the supposed letters by Shelley were forgeries. But the 'Introductory Essay', or 'Essay on Shelley' as it has come to be known, remains a notable expression of Browning's critical views on poets and poetry. See Critical Commentary, p. 171.